T0413840

"Whatever you do, do it well. Do it so well that when people see you do it, they will want to come back and see you do it again, and they will want to bring others and show them how well you do what you do."

—Walter E. Disney

Customer Loyalty and Supply Chain Management

Many business-to-business (B2B) managers think that customers act rationally and base decisions mostly on price; customer loyalty isn't considered. Companies outsource various activities, which enable them to improve efficiency, reduce costs, focus more on core competencies and improve their innovation capabilities. Supply chain management synchronises the efforts of all parties – particularly suppliers, manufacturers, retailers, dealers and customers – involved in achieving customers' needs. Despite much research, the relationship between customer loyalty and the supply chain strategy remains insufficiently explored and understood by practitioners and academics, while the theme has been extensively developed within marketing literature.

Customer Loyalty and Supply Chain Management is the result of years of work by the authors on different projects concerning the overlapping areas of supply chains, logistics and marketing, drawing a connection between the literature to provide a holistic picture of the customer loyalty framework. Emphasis is given to the B2B context, where recent research has provided some clues to support the fact that investment in operations, new technologies and organisational strategy have had a significant role in understanding B2B loyalty, particularly in the context of global supply chains. Moreover, the book provides a modernised and predictive model of B2B loyalty, showing a different methodological approach that aims at capturing the complexity of the phenomenon.

This book will be a useful resource for professionals and scholars from across the supply chain who are interested in exploring the dimension of customer loyalty in the challenging supplier and customer context.

Ivan Russo, Ph.D. is an Associate Professor at University of Verona. His research coalesces under the broad umbrella of supply chain management and marketing. He has published in the *Journal of Operations Management, Journal of Business Research, International Journal of Physical Distribution and Logistics Management, International Journal of Production Economics, Journal of Business and Industrial Marketing, Production Planning & Control, International Journal of Quality and Service Sciences* and *International Journal of Entrepreneurship and Small Business.*

Ilenia Confente, Ph.D. is an Assistant Professor at University of Verona. Her research interests range from B2B to digital marketing. She has published in *Journal of Business Research, Journal of Business and Industrial Marketing, International Journal of Tourism Research, International Journal of Quality and Service Sciences* and *International Journal of Entrepreneurship and Small Business.*

Routledge Studies in Business Organizations and Networks

For a full list of titles in this series, please visit www.routledge.com

Customer Loyalty and Supply Chain Management
Business-to-Business Customer Loyalty Analysis

Ivan Russo and Ilenia Confente

Routledge
Taylor & Francis Group

LONDON AND NEW YORK

First published 2017
by Routledge
2 Park Square, Milton Park, Abingdon, Oxon OX14 4RN

and by Routledge
711 Third Avenue, New York, NY 10017

Routledge is an imprint of the Taylor & Francis Group, an informa business

British Library Cataloguing-in-Publication Data
A catalogue record for this book is available from the British Library

Library of Congress Cataloging-in-Publication Data
A catalog record for this book has been requested

ISBN: 978-1-138-06084-5 (hbk)
ISBN: 978-1-315-16282-9 (ebk)

Typeset in Bembo
by Apex CoVantage, LLC

Contents

Figures

Tables

Boxes

Foreword

I was introduced to business as a sales representative for a large manufacturer of hospital diagnostics. While my company produced high-quality products, the intensely competitive nature of the industry taught me that great products and pricing alone do not keep customers buying. These are needed of course, but they are not sufficient. Rather, I learned to carefully cultivate my key accounts, ensuring that they received top-notch service on top of the great-quality products my firm offered. Ensuring that my top customers' orders were prioritized, filled completely, delivered on time or to exact specifications, and adjudicating any perceived errors in fulfillment, billing, etc., all became part of my job to ensure that my customers continued to order, and order more, from me instead of my competitors. Given that many of my accounts were hospital labs, I spent many evenings and weekend shifts working with lab personnel to help them to better use my products, solve any problems they may have had, and run interference for their priority orders. I remember reflecting after my first year on the job that this was not what I thought sales was about when I took that job after a stint as an operations officer on a ship in the U.S. Navy. In fact, it felt a lot like operations!

It was with this perspective on the importance of service – what I soon learned was called the "augmented product" – that I entered the Ph.D. program in what was then Marketing and Distribution at the University of Georgia. I found that my passion lay in exploring how the operational capabilities subsumed within the discipline that we now call supply chain management can be used to create a competitive advantage with customers. At the time this was not a very broadly accepted concept; rather, supply chain functions were linked primarily to cost performance. Frustratingly, still today I find myself engaged in rousing conversations with colleagues – and reviewers! – regarding the ability of supply chain management to impact an organization's top-line revenue growth.

Despite this general lack of recognition by the business academy, research conducted over the nearly 30 years of my academic career has identified the link between supply chain management service capabilities and industrial customers' purchase and repurchase intentions through heightened satisfaction and loyalty. In fact, shortly before I began my Ph.D. program, research conducted by

Douglas Lambert and Thomas Harrington found that purchasing managers for industrial customers considered what we now recognize as supply chain service to be among the most important elements of buying decisions, citing six of the top nine variables influencing purchasing decisions as being related to supply chain service elements.[1]

Since that time, both practice and research has borne out the robustness of the relationship between supply chain service and purchase decisions. As witness to this fact, a Chief Supply Chain Officer of a Fortune 100 firm (and Gartner Top 25 North American Supply Chain Firm) recently told me that her three key performance indicators were revenue growth, gross margin and cash-to-cash turnover – a far cry from the cost "box" that many relegate to supply chain performance. I believe that the link between supply chain performance and revenue growth through heightened satisfaction and loyalty will continue to increase in importance as industries reach maturity and venture into "commodity"-type competition that forces firms to seek alternative methods for differentiation. If product quality and features are viewed as highly similar, a marketing strategy that focuses on something other than product, price and promotions must be found in order to achieve strategic goals. Service provided by the supply chain has been shown to allow leading firms to focus not only on attracting new customers, but also on becoming closer to the ones they already have.

The scientist in me demands that such claims be backed up by sound evidence resulting from strong theory and rigorous method. Yet in 2017, we still do not have a roundly agreed upon definition of customer loyalty engendered from supply chain service. Neither have we fully plumbed the dimensionality and operationalization of the construct of supply chain customer loyalty. Beyond that, we also have not yet sufficiently demonstrated the linkage between supply chain service performance and purchase intentions so as to take our place at the table of business strategies that impact top-line revenue growth, costs/ margins and inventory turnover. This, to me, is a failing in supply chain research today that only becomes more glaring as business moves toward omnichannel fulfillment, with automation and predictive analytics breakthroughs that will enable innovative firms to achieve highly customized value provision for key customers.

This book seeks to right that wrong by providing a contemporary framework for exploring supply chain–related customer loyalty in business-to-business markets. In particular, the book will:

- Review previous research in B2B markets, including key concepts related to customer loyalty such as value, satisfaction, word of mouth, switching costs, trust, commitment, logistics service quality, reverse flow;
- Explore the main differences between B2C and B2B context;
- Further consider the implications of supply chain performance on customer loyalty in the context of information connectivity and online purchasing, big data analytics and multi- and omnichannel fulfillment;

- Identify new theory, methods and practices for measuring customer loyalty, including fuzzy set social science and qualitative comparative analysis and multiple regression analysis.

A mentor once told me that the role of business academia is to provide clear and specific definition of business concepts and to "separate truth from hype" by applying scientific method to precisely record relationships. This book seeks to deliver on those lofty goals in the domain of supply chain service and its impact on industrial customers' purchase intentions. I highly recommend that you read it!

Ted Stank
Harry and Vivienne Bruce Chair of Business Excellence
Professor of Supply Chain Management
Haslam College of Business
University of Tennessee

Note

1 Lambert D.M. and Harrington T.C. (1989) 'Establishing Customer Service Strategies Within the Marketing Mix: More Empirical Evidence', *Journal of Business Logistics*, 10(2), 44–72.

Preface

Succeeding in competitive business markets follows almost the same rules of sport, where several skills and capabilities are required to win the game. Satisfaction, continuous improvement, accountability, respect, teamwork, responsibility, time management, reaching success, problem solving, maintaining relationships, commitment and loyalty should all be learned from sports. Sports teach athletes to be committed and to get prepared for important games, to face new challenges, to learn from losses, to enjoy the wins.

A manager can be seen as an athlete, who needs to provide wisely the best performance and to deliver the best results, otherwise she/he will never overcome the competition to win the customers' commitment and loyalty. Thus, companies can achieve success by not only providing good products but also offering effective services or valuable solutions and developing good and long relationships with customers.

This book is the result of years of work on different projects concerning the overlapping areas of supply chains, logistics and marketing, in which the authors invested part of their research activity. Within this field, we specifically concentrated our efforts on providing a more modernised and predictive model of customer loyalty in a supply chain context adopting different methodologies.

Gaining loyalty in business-to-business (B2B) markets is very difficult and it poses unique challenges, from involving complicated distribution channel structures, to covering long distance between demand and supply, concentrating big accounts with many people influencing the relationship. Digitalisation of the business world is adding at the same time complexity but also an opportunity to provide a new way to keep in touch with the customers. Customer loyalty in the domain of B2B research encompasses many problems and challenges. One of the questions now facing managers in supply chain dyads and triads has become the following: 'what type of a relationship do I need to have with this supplier/buyer?' Understanding the value sought by other members in a supply chain network is critical because better alignment of objectives across companies can lead to competitive advantage and superior operational and financial performance. Indeed, loyalty is developed, integrated and coordinated along the supply chain members' activity nodes and links in the overall supply chain.

Despite much research on the subject in recent years, the relationship between customer loyalty and the supply chain strategy remains insufficiently explored and understood by practitioners and scholars, while the topic has been extensively developed within the marketing literature. Modern research in supply chain and logistics aims at integrating marketing notions and addressing the role of supply chain and logistics in delivering quality and improving customer service and satisfaction.

In this book, the emphasis will be given to this overlap, particularly considering the B2B context, where recent research has provided some clues to suspect that the investment in operations, new technologies and organisational strategy has been playing a significant role in understanding B2B loyalty, due to ever-increasing incidences of service failure stemming from the lengthening of global supply chains.

Moreover, understanding customer loyalty across a complex, longer and digital supply chain in the B2B context can be of particular help in today's changing and highly competitive business environment because it allows a way for understanding and anticipating customers' current and future needs in the era of omnichannel. In sum, the goal of this book is to analyse the several perspectives and ways to achieve customer loyalty in the B2B context.

Chapter 1 begins with a connection between marketing and supply chain literature in order to provide the whole picture of customer loyalty framework.

Chapter 2 supplies an extensive summary to previous works on B2B customer loyalty, trying to link it with some of its most recognised antecedents. Some of them are customer value, satisfaction, perceived switching costs, trust and commitment, managing returns flow, logistics service quality and word of mouth. The aim is to provide a clearer picture of B2B research on the drivers which build and enhance customer loyalty across the supply chain.

Chapter 3 focuses on the impact of digitalisation on B2B companies. Digitalisation has not only changed customers' purchasing behaviour and habits but it has of course provided companies with consistent new opportunities and threats. In the era of omnichannel, this chapter tries to summarise the main challenges this integration between offline and online has provided to both consumers and as a consequence companies.

Chapter 4 goes more in depth about the main changes and challenges supply chain management has faced with the advent of digitalisation and in particular the omnichannel environment, which has led to a significant rethink of supply chain operations, from inventory management to delivery, from organisation to IT systems.

Chapter 5 provides a more modernised and predictive model of B2B loyalty, showing a different methodological approach that aims at capturing the complexity of the phenomenon, measuring loyalty adopting different methods of analysis. Such analyses will be developed adopting two empirical studies. The final chapter concludes with some clues and suggestions for future research on customer loyalty across the supply chain.

This book can be useful for both scholars and practitioners as it covers an area that has not been studied in depth by previous publications and at the same time the style is straightforward and provides specific instructions for managers. In addition, it encompasses both traditional and virtual supply chains' context, providing a complete picture of the omnichannel environment, within which most of the companies are trying to compete and succeed.

Acknowledgments

This book has been possible only through the support and contributions from colleagues, practitioners and students across the years.

We would like to thank our research group on supply chain management and marketing at the University of Verona, particularly Antonio Borghesi for his original and fundamental support and inspiration concerning this stream of research, and Barbara Gaudenzi for her consistent daily support and understanding.

Our sincere gratitude goes to several influential colleagues who contributed by sharing with us their highly valuable thoughts, doubts, experiences and recommendations from working in the field of customer loyalty across the supply chain: Chad Autry, Robert Frankel, Diane Mollenkopf, Nicola Cobelli, David Gligor and Arch Woodside. The conceptual and methodological aspects of our research were significantly led by them.

Our special thanks to Ted Stank for taking time from his busy schedule for a final revision of the work and for his enduring support and guidance. We are honoured to have a foreword from one of the most influential scholars in the field.

This project could have not been realised without the continuous contact and sharing of knowledge with the hundreds of practitioners and managers we have met over the last 10 years through our research meetings, through which managers talked about the challenges they face every day to keep their customers loyal in a complex global context. Several examples in the book derive from our database of years of work with companies. We would like to acknowledge the LogiMaster Programme at the University of Verona, which represents the best place in Italy to interact with managers, scholars and master students working in the area of supply chain, logistics and marketing.

In addition, we would like to acknowledge the editor at Routledge, Kristina Abbott, and her colleagues for their assistance and their enthusiasm. We are also in debt to the three anonymous reviewers of the research monograph who made very valuable and constructive comments that helped improve the work significantly. Any errors that remain are our sole responsibility.

The writing of this book was challenging on many levels and involved several sacrifices for the people who live with us. Ivan would like to dedicate this book to his wife, Chiara, for her consistent understanding and support – there was never any need to explain why Ivan was writing another book or paper. He also thanks his son, Lorenzo, and his daughter, Martina, who just smiled and laughed when Ivan tried to explain what he was doing, but who quickly realised the role of the supply chain in delivering toys to their house. Ivan would like to acknowledge his co-author, Ilenia, who shared this research topic with him for several years and whose passion and determination always drove him to achieve more.

Ilenia would like to thank her one-year-old son, Andrea, from whom she has taken time out to focus on this work. Thank you to Andrea for having completed her life and for his happy-go-lucky way of seeing the world. She thanks her husband, Giovanni, a pillar of strength and support through these busy and hard times. She would like to thank her co-author and point of reference, Ivan, for his perseverance and enthusiasm in approaching every research project.

Thanks, finally, to our past and present students at the college who have shared their thoughts and doubts with us about supply chains, logistics and marketing; they inspire us at the start of every semester.

Ivan Russo and Ilenia Confente
February, 2017
University of Verona (Italy)

1 Achieving integration between supply chain management and marketing

Research in business-to-business marketing

Companies can achieve success and customer retention not only through the provision of good products but also by offering effective services and developing good relationships with supply chain members. Many business-to-business (B2B) managers believe that their customers act rationally and base decisions mostly on price; customer loyalty is not a consideration. However, achieving loyalty in B2B markets is difficult and poses unique challenges. It often involves complicated distribution channel structures – frequently having to navigate a significant gap between demand and supply, and manage large accounts with many people who influence the relationship. To add complexity but also opportunities to the issue, digitalisation of the business world provides new ways to keep in touch with customers (Lingqvist, Plotkin and Stanley, 2015). Most managers fail to recognise that the same customers who require a value proposition for purchases also require a different set of attributes for other products for which they will be prepared to pay more. Defining what the customers want and how best to engage them requires tailored solutions and a higher level of analysis across the supply chain. Customer loyalty in the B2B context is much more complex than is often reported (Hines, 2014).

A recent Bain & Company survey of executive-level managers in B2B industries throughout 11 countries shows that 68% of respondents believe customers are less loyal than they used to be. Moreover, the same survey reveals that earning loyalty in B2B markets faces unique business problems, often involving complex channel structures, concentrated buyer communities or large accounts, and continuous shifting of perceived value (Michels and Dullweber, 2014). Not all executives treat customer loyalty as something different from customer satisfaction. Customer satisfaction is just an attitude at a moment in time, while loyalty is actual behaviour that results in multiple buying cycles over time.

The term B2B indicates, firstly, all the relationships that a company has with its suppliers for procurement activities, planning and monitoring of production or support in product development activities. Moreover, it also describes the relationships that the company has with professional clients or other companies that are connected at different points of the production chain. A B2B relationship usually involves more than two or three individuals; all these people have different needs and backgrounds. The principle behind 'relationship marketing' is that the organisation should consciously strive to develop marketing strategies to maintain and strengthen customer loyalty (Reichheld, 1994). Conceptualising and analysing these marketing situations requires different research approaches that deal with purchasing complexity and customer prospect heterogeneity. In sum, it is a complex and heterogeneous business context. Second, in a B2B market, work experiences, production and engineering are essentials. Thus, companies that have a technical background but no business experience are less useful in professional development processes. Third, in a B2B context there is generally a lack of data availability; data for B2B contexts are rarer and more difficult to collect for scholars than are data for business-to-consumer (B2C) contexts. Thus, the domain of B2B research encompasses many open questions. Studying the B2B market could be useful for building theories related to different disciplines, but B2B research also faces heterogeneity in the units of analyses and thus can reveal different theoretical perspectives (Håkansson and Snehota, 1989; Reid and Plank, 2000; Gummesson and Polese, 2009; Vargo and Lusch, 2011). Early marketing was simply an application of economic theory, while business relationships were a combination of economic, organisational and social factors. Concepts like reciprocity, mutuality and trust have since acquired a new importance and they are closely connected to B2B research.

This view is clearly in contrast with the guidelines of economic theory, which focuses on the lowest production costs and maximum profits in the exchange. Economic theory researchers were primarily concerned with consumer markets, and the main goal was to connect consumers to society using, to begin with, economic theory, then later, social theory, and then organisational behaviour theory (Alderson and Cox, 1948; Alderson, 1965). Later, the line of reasoning changed slowly following the idea that customers are also important and could contribute to the creation of value. It was not until some years later that the first course in industrial marketing was developed at Harvard Business School by Ray Corey, who published *Industrial Marketing: Cases and Concepts* (Corey, 1962). Later Peter Drucker argued:

> What the customer thinks he or she is buying, what he or she considers value, is decisive – it determines what a business is, what it produces, and whether it will prosper . . . Customers are the foundation of a business and keep it in existence. To supply the wants and needs of a customer, society entrusts wealth-producing resources to the business enterprise.
>
> (1974 p. 57)

A notable contribution to research came from The Industrial Marketing and Purchasing Group, which was formed in the 1970s between five European research groups from France, Germany, Italy, Sweden and the UK. The approach was basically to see B2B marketing as an ongoing interaction between buyers and sellers; this approach is based on relationship marketing and implies the buyers and sellers are dependent on each other and create value for both sides (Håkansson and Snehota, 1989; Snehota and Håkansson, 1995; Gadde, Håkansson and Persson, 2010; Cantù, Corsaro, Fiocca and Tunisini, 2013). Then, in the 1980s, many marketers moved from the term 'industrial' goods marketing to 'business' marketing and, finally, by the 1990s, 'business marketing' frequently displaced 'industrial marketing' and the label 'B2B marketing' became very popular (Hunt, 2013). In recent years, B2B marketing has become a decision-making activity directed at satisfying customers' needs and wants. Gradually moving towards B2B markets, it also required an analytical understanding of all members involved in the value chain.

Compared with B2C, B2B marketers focus on fewer and more varied customers, using more complex and typically oriented sales processes. The presence of a few powerful customers means that many common tools and data used in B2C are inappropriate for the B2B market. In addition, B2C transactions still occur through common channels; this is in opposition to B2B transactions, which are more private and direct. Thus, the key distinguishing feature of B2B is that the customer is an organisation rather than an individual customer, in contrast to consumer markets, which focus only on the relationship between the supplier and the final customer.

In sum, consumers, after all, care deeply about brands and are more readily influenced by advertising, media messages, special deals, coupons and word of mouth (WOM) through online or offline avenues, and they can switch from one brand to the next with little cost. Meanwhile, business purchase managers and supply managers conduct significant research, examine specifications, follow a formal buying or procurement process, experience high switching costs, and usually worry most about functionality, volumes and price (Lingqvist et al., 2015). Finally, in the B2B context, decision-makers buy with the ultimate goal of adding value at less cost to move the products from upstream of the value chain to downstream.

Supply chain management: a pillar for business-to-business marketing

Alderson and Martin (1965) stated that the key to maximising organisational wealth was to integrate the diffused transactional and transvectional demand and supply elements in the distribution channel to create value. A transvection is, in a sense, the outcome of a series of transactions beginning with raw materials and ending with a product at the consumer level. Alderson's transvection (1965) presages what is now referred to as 'supply chain management' (SCM), incorporating the theory of marketing (Hunt, 2013). According to Esper, Ellinger, Stank, Flint and Moon (2010), Alderson demonstrates how the flow of information and product alteration or transformation results in transvections, or an entire system of exchanges that are premises of the need of demand and supply management integration. Indeed, over the last 20 years there has been a significant directional change in both marketing practice and theory with regards to the idea of relationship marketing – that is, establishing, developing and maintaining successful relational exchanges (Morgan and Hunt, 1994). Today, the relevance of relationships between customers and suppliers is extensively recognised in the business literature.

Interest in the supply chain concept has received considerable attention since the 1980s, especially since firms have realised that the market's evolution towards a reduction in lead time and more responsive supply would drive them into organisation isolation from the other members of the chain. SCM thus plays a key role in exploring such relationships across the supply chain.

However, even with great interest in the topic, there is no definitional consensus for SCM among scholars and practitioners. We view the supply chain as:

> The systemic, strategic coordination of the traditional business functions and the tactics across these business functions within a particular company and across businesses within the supply chain, for the purposes of improving the long-term performance of the individual companies and the supply chain as a whole.
>
> (Mentzer et al., 2001, p. 11)

The main idea is to consider supply chain as a flow in which the members have only the function to choose the physical flow of goods. New research and theories in addition to those concerning the typical members of a supply chain have considered other members who have a supportive and secondary role but who are equally important.

A relevant contribution comes from the network perspective used by Carter, Rogers and Choi (2015), which defines the supply chain as a set of nodes and links. A node represents a member of the chain with the ability to maximise its own profit while respecting the limits in which it operates. A link consists of the transactions between two nodes. Thus, the supply chain is a complex and dynamic system that is difficult to forecast and control. Each node in the supply chain manages its own resources to obtain a profit and coordinates its actions with the purpose of achieving visibility upstream towards its suppliers and downstream to its customers. However, as we have seen, other members can influence the performance of a specific node; beyond their visibility range, an agent is subject to the decisions of the other members and cannot exercise control over them. For every supply chain, the mechanism is the same: to analyse a single situation, we must refer to the focal company. The case of an individual agent and of the focal firm can differ from one another based on the typology of goods or the mode of transportation. However, the specific case is important to identify in order to analyse a supply chain and a point of reference. Each agent can be involved in a unique supply chain or in many. While Mentzer et al. (2001) analyse the complexity of supply chains, identifying numerous actors with increasing complexity, Carter et al. (2015), concentrate more on the nodes and links of the supply chain, where customers and suppliers often connected not as a linear chain but as a network. In particular, the model shown in

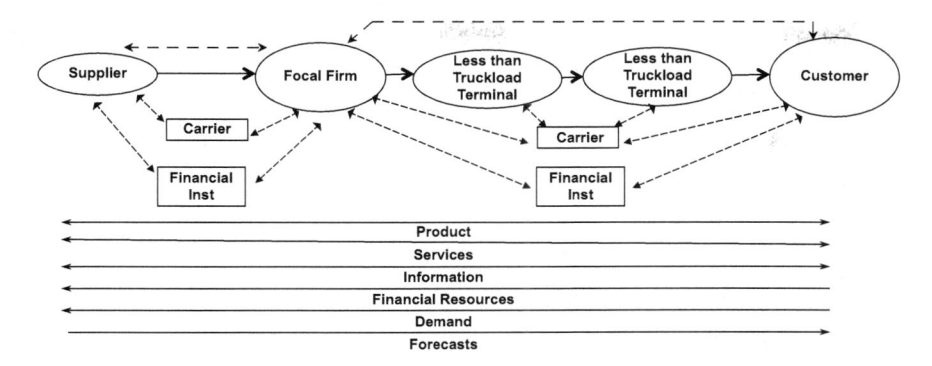

Figure 1.1 The physical and support supply chain as a network

Adapted from Carter et al. (2015)

Figure 1.1 illustrates the dynamics of carrier activity. The carrier is considered as either a physical or a support node, demonstrating a more complete framework of how value-adding activities are organised in a supply chain. In that case a product moves from the focal agent (node) through warehouse terminals to the focal agent's customer in the physical supply chain.

SCM coordinates business functions within and between organisations and their channel partners. SCM strives to provide goods and services that fulfil customer demand responsively, efficiently and sustainably. Further, it includes functions such as demand forecasting, purchasing or call sourcing, customer relationship management and logistics. Thus, supply chain perspectives reflect knowledge and operational capabilities through information coordination and collaboration across organisations throughout the service ecosystem. When supply chains are not integrated in the product, information and financial flow, or are not appropriately organised and managed, the results are inefficient and resources are wasted.

Thus, over recent years the increased interest in SCM can be summarised as:

- increasing consumer expectations of product quality and customer service coupled with local and regional preferences across multiple marketing channels;
- increased globalisation, which has created a geographical decomposition of the value chain, with the most common phenomena being global sourcing and offshoring;
- great environmental uncertainty resulting from the huge impact of technology and digitalisation, competition, different governmental rules and regulations, macro-economics, world geopolitical dynamics and rising levels of material scarcity for raw materials; and
- the trend towards reducing lead time and increasing services, which require closer relationships and coordination between the members of the supply chain, mainly in the era of e-commerce.

These dynamics will affect the efficiency (i.e., cost reduction) and the effectiveness (i.e., customer service) of supply chains designed to create time, place and form utility to improve the customers' commitment.

Additionally, we are in an era of global supply chains comprising a worldwide network of suppliers, manufacturers, warehouses, distribution centres and retailers through which raw materials are acquired, transformed and delivered to customers. Moreover, changing demographics, with middle-class growth in China, India and Vietnam, and expectations of higher growth for some countries in Africa, have led global companies to mine these new markets for growth and profitability. Nowadays 54% of the worldwide population lived in an urban area, which is expected to rise to over 66% by mid-century (United Nations, 2015); this will be a challenge for companies and third party logistics due to an increase in online shopping will require more urban logistics premises to fulfil late cut-off deliveries.

Today, supply chain managers must develop competencies that allow them to understand complexity, anticipate major changes and trends and adapt to those changes as needed.

Consequently, such a context leads companies in one country to depend on companies from other countries, either to supply material or to market their products. This strategy also renders organisations potentially less responsive, more dependent on long-term forecasts and vulnerable to the delay and change of demand. Globalisation has set up large systems of trading partners that span vast distances. Vertical integration, once commonplace, is now rare. While outsourcing has cost advantages, it also has a downside – lack of control and oversight; globalising the marketplace and the need of logistics service providers to render logistics services on an international scale requires intercultural management competencies. These are significant challenges for retaining customer loyalty.

However, the diverse framework shows a greater focus on supplier–customer dyads, where there are activities, actors and resources with an increasing interest in marketing research (Mele and Polese, 2011; Vargo and Lusch, 2011; Grönroos and Helle, 2012). This context also exists for supply chain research, where firms can benefit from long-term relationships leading to long-term customer retention (Ganesan, 1994; Terpend, Tyler, Krause and Handfield, 2008). Further, supply chain relationships can be a stable source of competitive advantage because of their ability to create barriers to competition (Golicic and Mentzer, 2006). Several studies emphasise the importance of building and maintaining relationships in business-to-business marketing (Lapierre, Filiatrault and Chebat, 1999; Jacob and Ulaga, 2008; Lapierre, Terpend et al., 2008). In a supplier–customer relationship, value facilitation can be regarded as a prerequisite or foundation for value creation and, thus, a reason for customers to seek a relationship with a supplier. The question now facing managers in supply chain dyads and triads has become 'what type of a relationship do I need to have with this supplier/buyer?' Relationship value in a B2B context is a dynamic process where the nature and characteristics of the value sought are constantly changing across different supply chain members.

Thus the advantages of an individual firm are often linked to the network of relationships in which the firm is embedded and where that firm is perceived to deliver value to the rest of the network. Understanding the value sought by other members in a supply chain network is critical because better alignment of objectives across companies can lead to competitive advantage and superior operational and financial performance. Indeed, loyalty is developed, integrated and coordinated along the supply chain members' activity nodes and links in the overall supply chain.

The effectiveness of the supply chain is measured when the customers decide where, what and how to buy a product. To do so, there is a need for strong integration of functions such as marketing, logistics, operations and purchasing within and across multiple firms (Frankel, Bolumole, Eltantawy, Paulraj and Gundlach, 2008; Matthyssens, Bocconcelli, Pagano and Quintens, 2016). Firms that effectively manage the supply chain combine functions, processes and activities across organisations, ultimately resulting in benefits such as value creation, increased efficiency and enhanced customer satisfaction (Lambert, García-Dastugue and Croxton, 2008; Stock, Boyer and Harmon, 2010; Kozlenkova, Hult, Lund, Mena and Kekec, 2015). Supply chain integration focuses also on inter-firm integration (i.e., a firm's relationships with its suppliers and its customers) as well as internal integration. This aspect is often referred to as 'cross-functional integration' and is usually dyadic in nature, referring to a process of interdepartmental interaction and collaboration in which multiple functions work together in a cooperative manner to arrive at mutually acceptable outcomes for their organisation. The integration achieves a superior supply chain performance that can also produce a competitive advantage to increase revenues and to control expenses and profit margins. Recently Lambert and Enz (2017) required more research to identify deficiencies in the capabilities of each function as well as in the customer and supplier networks in order to develop capabilities that support the implementation the management of the supply chain.

The collaborative programmes exist where supplier and customer share supply and demand forecasts and schedules to reduce demand variability. The purpose is to migrate them to a continuous replenishment flow model, which is a high-value model that generates higher levels of customer loyalty. Moreover, new fulfilment and supply chain strategies have emerged as companies have responded to the changing marketplace by developing alternative solutions (i.e., agile, responsiveness, lean). However, no one-size-fits-all approach exists and the supply chain strategy should be evaluated and tailored to specific company requirements. In addition, to enhance their competitiveness, many companies outsource some activities, which enables them to improve their operational efficiency, reduce costs, focus more on their core competencies and improve their innovation capabilities. Customers whose buying behaviour follows a regular, predictable pattern should be invited to participate in collaborative programmes.

Whereas logistics and SCM have traditionally referred to the physical flow connecting production with customers, more recent research in logistics aims at integrating marketing notions and addressing the role of logistics in delivering quality and improving customer service and satisfaction. One of marketing's main concerns is delivering value to the end user, and efficient supply chains are perhaps the most imperative for the marketing function, as Ellis argues:

> When firms make mistakes anywhere within a supply chain, the effects can ripple through the chain in both directions. These effects include disruption to production, forecasting errors, inventory imbalances, stock-outs or damaged goods, all of which usually result in increased costs that may have to be passed on to end users, thus reducing their satisfaction and loyalty.
>
> (Ellis, 2011, p. 109)

Thus, logisticians and marketers need to adopt the role of marketing to both internal and external customers from the beginning of supply chain relationships. This is because logisticians have a unique ability to see, understand, anticipate, adapt and design solutions for logistics-relevant customer changes that marketing and sales are not able to recognise (Mentzer, Flint and Hult, 2001). However, because of the higher complexity of a multinational context, which makes it more difficult for customers to evaluate suppliers and fosters feelings of ambiguity and risk, it would be very useful for suppliers to discover the customer's unexpressed and latent needs as well (Corsaro, Ramos, Henneberg and Naudé, 2012).

SCM spans a broader domain than simply business procurement or logistics functions or production units; thus, it would be a mistake to limit a firm's view of SCM to its functions and physical spaces. Handling the supply chain is a complex endeavour that requires both cross-functional processes and the management of relationships within and across organisations to build up the source-to-consumer network. Supply chain integration can ensure a smoother, more efficient flow of products, and can enable access to third-party resources and capabilities that would be too costly to build internally.

Demand and supply integration (DSI) is presented in the literature as a firm-level strategy for balancing the needs of customers with the capacity and capabilities of upstream suppliers (Esper et al., 2010). In other words, we are in an era of SCM where seamlessly integrated groups of firms are uniting multiple functional efforts around a singular goal of delivering optimum value at the entire supply chain's lowest landed costs (Autry, Goldsby and Bell, 2012). In the search to achieve excellence, firms adopt organisational models that are focused on the highest level of efficiency, efficacy, flexibility and reactivity; the goal is to share information in an enlarged firm structure in which the supply chain's actors have a role. Dynamism and reactiveness can make companies competitive in the global markets, but this happens only when there are integrated systems and shared information throughout the chain.

There is a growing interest in the idea of integrating demand and supply in a single process to engage all functions in creating aligned, forward-looking plans and in making decisions that will optimise resources and organisational goals.

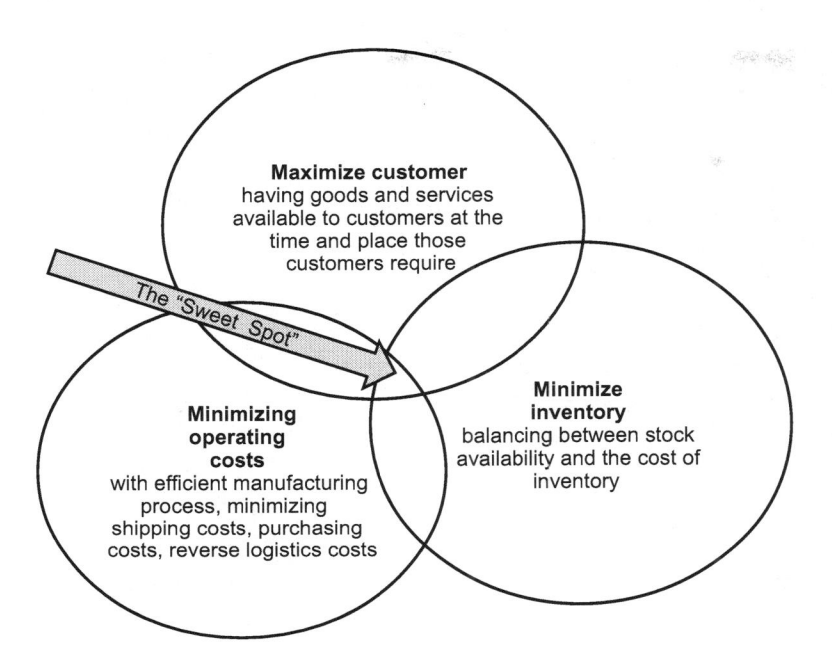

Figure 1.2 How demand and supply integration works
Adapted from Moon (2016)

However, research suggests that most companies still do not know how to serve their most important customers in a way that maximises the value to their customers and to themselves. That is, customer requirements must be well understood within the firm; this understanding must then be disseminated, interpreted and applied to fulfilment activities with respect to both real-time demand as well as ongoing supply capacity constraints. In this way, value is not so much created for the customer, but is more co-created with the customer and supplier. Scholars have found that value requirements often vary significantly across customers or segments of choice, demanding cost efficiency in some cases and product and service differentiation in others (Tate, Mollenkopf, Stank and Da Silva, 2015; Autry and Moon, 2016). Moving into the supply chain realm, the emphasis on co-creation of value drives organisational attention towards those activities that add to customer value, and moves attention away from activities that do not contribute to superior customer value. Thus, the ideal structure of DSI presents three main principles: it must be demand-driven, collaborative and disciplined (Moon, 2016). When these principles are covered, the 'magic' of DSI can be realised in a so-called 'sweet spot', finding the right balance between customer service, inventory management and operation costs.

An effective and efficient supply chain helps companies to pass along increased value to the end-customers and improve performance outcomes for the firm;

this places marketing at the centre of SCM strategy and operations (Kozlenkova et al., 2015) to keep the customer loyal. One of the most challenging outcomes to achieve is customer loyalty, a key point that concerns managers when considering how to improve relationships with their clients. The topic is not only relevant in the B2C context but also in the B2B context where firms enter into relationship with suppliers and service providers. Consequently, an important focus of supply chain research that is not just around collaborative relationships with select trading partners but is also an important strategic outcome for firms is the realisation of customer loyalty (Davis-Sramek, Mentzer and Stank, 2008).

Obtaining a thorough understanding of customer loyalty in a B2B context is a prerequisite for the following chapters. Thus, the development of customer loyalty research within the framework of marketing and supply chain context will be presented in the first part of our work. The next chapter aims to present a selection of the most important literature about customer loyalty in the B2B setting before both the consequences and the antecedents of customer loyalty are portrayed. It introduces best-practice knowledge of the topic and underlines the gaps that still exist. To investigate the linkage between customer loyalty and other dimensions (such as switching costs, customer service, customer satisfaction, customer value, WOM and logistics service), the issue is divided into macro categories.

Despite much research on the subject in recent years, the relationship between customer loyalty – understood as a buyer's intent to repurchase from a given supplier – and the supply chain strategy remains insufficiently explored and understood by practitioners and academics, while the theme has been extensively developed within the marketing literature. Within this context, our book aims at filling this gap, drawing a connection between marketing and supply chain literature to provide a complete picture of the customer loyalty framework. In particular, emphasis will be given to the B2B context, where recent research suggests that investment in operations, new technologies and organisational strategies have been playing a significant role in understanding B2B loyalty. This can be linked to the ever-increasing incidences of service failure stemming from the lengthening of global supply chains.

In the next chapter, we would like to include an extensive summary of previous works in the field. Moreover, to provide a clearer picture of B2B loyalty across the supply chain, we will describe in depth several aspects that potentially enhance loyalty, such as value, satisfaction, perceived switching costs, outsourcing decisions, managing returns flow, omnichannel strategies and WOM. It is not a goal of this book to investigate antecedents of loyalty with a high impact on customer loyalty, such as price, brand reputation, product quality or incentives (i.e., benefits, investments, rewards). Rather, the specific analysis is to show how supply chain and logistics should keep and enhance loyalty through managing internal and external product flow across the supply chain. From the supplier-focused perspective, customer loyalty is a bundle of measures that deliver success in keeping the customer loyal, while the customer-focus approach takes into consideration customer attitudes and intentions in the context of loyalty. Thus, it is important for suppliers to understand the antecedents that may determine repurchase and loyalty overall, listening to each customer and not to the network as a whole. A third perspective identified is the relationship-focused perspective, which directly examines the relationship between suppliers and customers. In our book, the dominant perspective uses the customer's perception as the central driver to analyse the more appropriate configuration of antecedents across the supply chain to keep customers loyal. Finally, our objective is to provide a more modernised and predictive model of customer loyalty, in particular in the B2B context.

References

Alderson, W. (1965) Dynamic marketing behavior: a functionalist theory of marketing, Homewood, IL: R. D. Irwin.

Alderson, W. and Cox, R. (1948) 'Towards a theory of marketing', *Journal of Marketing*, 13(2), 137–152.

Alderson, W. and Martin, M. W. (1965) 'Toward a formal theory of transactions and transvections', *Journal of Marketing Research*, 2(2), 117–127.

Autry, C. W., Goldsby, J. T. and Bell, E. J. (2012) *Global macro trends and their impact on supply chain management*, Upper Saddle River, NJ: Pearson Education.

Autry, C. W. and Moon, M. A. (2016) Achieving supply chain integration: connecting the supply chain inside and out for competitive advantage, Old Tappan, NJ: FT Press.

Cantù, C., Corsaro, D., Fiocca, R. and Tunisini, A. (2013) 'IMP studies: a bridge between tradition and innovation', *Industrial Marketing Management*, 42(7), 1007–1016.

Carter, C. R., Rogers, D. S. and Choi, T. Y. (2015) 'Toward the theory of the supply chain', *Journal of Supply Chain Management*, 51(2), 89–97.

Corey, E. R. (1962) *Industrial marketing: cases and concepts*, Englewood Cliffs, NJ: Prentice-Hall.

Corsaro, D., Ramos, C., Henneberg, S. C. and Naudé, P. (2012) 'The impact of network configurations on value constellations in business markets – the case of an innovation network', *Industrial Marketing Management*, 41(1), 54–67. doi:10.1016/j.indmarman.2011.11.017.

Davis-Sramek, B., Mentzer, J. T. and Stank, T. P. (2008) 'Creating consumer durable retailer customer loyalty through order fulfillment service operations', *Journal of Operations Management*, 26(6), 781–797.

Drucker, P. F. (1974) *Management: tasks, responsibilities, practices'*, London: William Heinemann Ltd.

Ellis, N. (2011) *Business-to-business marketing*, New York, NY: Oxford University Press.

Esper, T. L., Ellinger, A. E., Stank, T. P., Flint, D. J. and Moon, M. (2010) 'Demand and supply integration: a conceptual framework of value creation through knowledge management', *Journal of the Academy of Marketing Science*, 38(1), 5–18. doi:10.1007/s11747-009-0135-3.

Frankel, R., Bolumole, Y. A., Eltantawy, R. A., Paulraj, A. and Gundlach, G. T. (2008) 'The domain and scope of SCM's foundational disciplines – insights and issues to advance research', *Journal of Business Logistics*, 29(1), 1–30.

Gadde, L.-E., Håkansson, H. and Persson, G. (2010) *Supply network strategies*, Chichester: John Wiley & Sons.

Ganesan, S. (1994) 'Determinants of long-term orientation in buyer-seller relationships', *Journal of Marketing*, 58(2), 1–19.

Golicic, S. L. and Mentzer, J. T. (2006) 'An empirical examination of relationship magnitude', *Journal of Business Logistics*, 27(1), 81–108.

Grönroos, C. and Helle, P. (2012) 'Return on relationships: conceptual understanding and measurement of mutual gains from relational business engagements', *Journal of Business & Industrial Marketing*, 27(5), 344–359. doi:10.1108/08858621211236025.

Gummesson, E. and Polese, F. (2009) 'B2B is not an island!', *Journal of Business & Industrial Marketing*, 24(5/6), 337–350.

Håkansson, H. and Snehota, I. (1989) 'No business is an island: the network concept of business strategy', *Scandinavian Journal of Management*, 5(3), 187–200.

Hines, T. (2014) Supply chain strategies: demand driven and customer focused, London: Routledge.

Hunt, S. D. (2013) 'A general theory of business marketing: RA theory, Alderson, the ISBM framework, and the IMP theoretical structure', *Industrial Marketing Management*, 42(3), 283–293.

Jacob, F. and Ulaga, W. (2008) 'The transition from product to service in business markets: an agenda for academic inquiry', *Industrial Marketing Management*, 37(3), 247–253. doi:10.1016/j.indmarman.2007.09.009.

Kozlenkova, I. V., Hult, G. T. M., Lund, D. J., Mena, J. A. and Kekec, P. (2015) 'The role of marketing channels in supply chain management', *Journal of Retailing*, 91(4), 586–609.

Lambert, D. M., & Enz, M. G. (2017). 'Issues in supply chain management: Progress and potential', *Industrial Marketing Management*, 62(April 2017), 1–16.

Lambert, D. M., García-Dastugue, S. J., and Croxton, K. L. (2008) 'The role of logistics managers in the cross-functional implementation of supply chain management', *Journal of Business Logistics*, 29(1), 113–132.

Lapierre, J., Filiatrault, P. and Chebat, J. C. (1999) 'Value strategy rather than quality strategy: a case of business-to-business professional services', *Journal of Business Research*, 45(2), 235–246.

Lingqvist, O., Plotkin, C. L. and Stanley, J. (2015) 'Do you really understand how your business customers buy', *McKinsey Quarterly*, February, 1–11.

Matthyssens, P., Bocconcelli, R., Pagano, A. and Quintens, L. (2016) 'Aligning marketing and purchasing for new value creation', *Industrial Marketing Management*, 52, 60–73.

Mele, C. and Polese, F. (2011) 'Key dimensions of service systems in value-creating networks', in H. Demirkan, J. Spohrer and V. Krishna (eds), *The science of service systems*, New York: Springer, 37–59.

Mentzer, J. T., DeWitt, W., Keebler, J. S., Min, S., Nix, N. W., Smith, C. D. and Zacharia, Z. G. (2001) 'Defining supply chain management', *Journal of Business Logistics*, 22(2), 1–25.

Mentzer, J. T., Flint, D. J. and Hult, G. T. M. (2001) 'Logistics service quality as a segment-customized process', *Journal of Marketing*, 65(4), 82–104.

Michels, D. and Dullweber, A. (2014) *Do your B2B customers promote your business?* San Francisco, CA: Bain & Company.

Moon, M. (2016) 'Achieving demand and supply integration', in Chad W. Autry and Mark A. Moon (eds), *Achieving supply chain integration: connecting the supply chain inside and out for competitive advantage*, Old Tappan, NJ: Pearson FT Press.

Morgan, R. M. and Hunt, S. D. (1994) 'The commitment-trust theory of relationship marketing', *Journal of Marketing*, 20–38.

Reichheld, F. F. (1994) 'Loyalty and the renaissance of marketing', *Marketing Management*, 2(4), 10.

Reid, D. A. and Plank, R. E. (2000) 'Business marketing comes of age: a comprehensive review of the literature', *Journal of Business-to-Business Marketing*, 7(2–3), 9–186.

Snehota, I. and Håkansson, H. (1995) *Developing relationships in business networks*, London, UK: Routledge.

Stock, J. R., Boyer, S. L. and Harmon, T. (2010) 'Research opportunities in supply chain management', *Journal of the Academy of Marketing Science*, 38(1), 32–41.

Tate, W. L., Mollenkopf, D., Stank, T. and Da Silva, A. L. (2015) 'Integrating supply and demand', *MIT Sloan Management Review*, 56(4), 16.

Terpend, R., Tyler, B. B., Krause, D. R. and Handfield, R. B. (2008) 'Buyer – supplier relationships: derived value over two decades', *Journal of Supply Chain Management*, 44(2), 28–55.

United Nations Department of Social and Economic Affairs. (2014) *World's population increasingly urban with more than half living in urban areas*. Available at http://www.un.org/en/development/desa/news/population/world-urbanization-prospects-2014.html.

Vargo, S. L. and Lusch, R. F. (2011) 'It's all B2B . . . and beyond: toward a systems perspective of the market', *Industrial Marketing Management*, 40(2), 181–187.

2 Customer loyalty in the business-to-business context

Customer loyalty background

Business scholars have long proposed that firms with a good understanding of the sources of customer loyalty can gain market advantages (Wind, 1970; Palmatier, Scheer and Steenkamp, 2007) such as increased revenues, lower costs and increased profitability, to name a few (Dick and Basu, 1994; Gundlach, Achrol and Mentzer, 1995; Christopher, 2016). Loyalty is a central concept in the relationship marketing paradigm because customer retention contributes to lower customer acquisition costs and thus positively affects the firm's profitability and market share (Anderson, Fornell and Lehmann, 1994). Traditionally, customer loyalty has been defined as buyers' deeply held commitment to stick with a product, service, brand or organisation in the future, despite new opportunities or competitive situations that influence switching (Oliver, 1999). Morgan and Hunt suggest that 'loyalty [is] increasingly similar to our conceptualisation of commitment' (1994, p. 23). Thus, this dimension is like relationship commitment in buyer-seller interactions where customers have a permanent intent to maintain long-term relationships (Anderson and Weitz, 1992).

According to various scholars in the field of industrial marketing, customer loyalty has been studied as a relationship between customer and supplier (Dwyer, Schurr and Oh, 1987; Biong, 1993; Innis and La Londe, 1994; Bloemer and De Ruyter, 1999; Ellinger, Daugherty and Plair, 1999; Davis and Mentzer, 2006; Wallenburg, Cahill, Michael Knemeyer and Goldsby, 2011; Blocker, Flint, Myers and Slater, 2011; Watson, Beck, Henderson and Palmatier, 2015). As research progressed, scholars suggested that loyalty might be bi-dimensional, incorporating both attitudinal and behavioural loyalty (Day, 1969). Attitudinal loyalty represents a buyer's emotional or psychological commitment to a brand, provider or a supplier (Rauyruen and Miller, 2007; Cater and Cater, 2009), while behavioural loyalty captures a buyer's intention to repurchase from the same provider in the past, present or future (Stank, Goldsby and Vickery, 1999; Homburg and Giering, 2001; Hewett, Money and Sharma, 2002; Guenzi and Pelloni, 2004; Davis-Sramek, Mentzer and Stank, 2008). Subsequently, researchers adopted this two-dimensional view, often referred to as composite loyalty (Oliver, Rust and Varki, 1997; Dick and Basu, 1994; Blocker et al., 2011). Some scholars exploring business relationships test for both affective commitment (attitudinal) and repurchase intention constructs, which coincide with the two loyalty dimensions mentioned above (Gundlach et al., 1995; Verhoef, 2003; Lam, Shankar, Erramilli and Murthy, 2004; Blocker et al., 2011). Attitudinal loyalty has been extensively explored compared with behavioural loyalty, particularly in relation to its antecedents. In contrast, when considering the outcomes of loyalty as WOM or financial performance, behavioural loyalty affects performance more compared with attitudinal loyalty.

In summary, loyalty has been defined in terms of repeat purchasing, long-term commitment, intention to continue the relationship and likelihood of not switching from a given supplier (Davis-Sramek et al., 2008). In relation to repurchase intentions, customer loyalty includes customers' perceptions of continuity expectations, such as business relationship renewal. Scholars have acknowledged the multidimensional nature of customer loyalty; however, a consensus has not been reached regarding the dimensions that should be incorporated in its measurement.

Recently, Watson et al. (2015, p. 26) stated that 'customer loyalty is a collection of attitudes aligned with a series of purchase behaviours that systematically favour one entity over competing entities' (p. 804). Further, they underline the systematic divergence between conceptualisation (What is customer loyalty?), measurement of loyalty (How is it measured?) and, finally, the implications for strategy and performance (What actually matters?).

Table 2.1 provides a list of major studies that have discussed loyalty in the B2B context in the major journals of marketing and supply chain/logistics. The majority captured the data from the customer's side of the dyad. Thus, in our business context we define loyalty in terms of a customer's intent to repurchase and to do business with the supplier in the future.

Keeping loyal customers means having customers whose lifetime value is greater than that of a customer who seldom purchases company products and services and is likely to easily switch to another supplier or service provider. The importance of customer loyalty is summarised by the concept of the 'lifetime value' of the customers. Customer lifetime value looks at a customer's financial value to the firm based on predicted future costs and transactions; measuring the lifetime value of a customer requires an estimation of the likely cash flow from a customer over the life of his or her relationship and loyalty with the firm (Gupta et al., 2006; Kumar, 2008; Ritter and Andersen, 2014). In a few words, if customers remain loyal to a supplier, their lifetime value can be enhanced.

Understanding the antecedents and the reasons for customer loyalty should help in developing the most appropriate supply chain strategy. That is a great effort but it deserves higher attention on customer complaints and customer dissatisfaction. Typically, a company takes more energies in getting customers rather than in keeping them. Consequently, many practitioners have failed to comprehend the importance of customer loyalty as a driver of profitability and hence have tended to concentrate just on short-term perspective with the aim of increasing market share (Christopher and Peck, 2012).

Table 2.1 Main definitions of customer loyalty in the B2B context

Reference	Context	Loyalty Definition
Biong (1993), *European Journal of Marketing*	A survey of supermarket contexts was used to study the way in which suppliers use the marketing mix variable to influence the satisfaction and loyalty of retailers.	Loyalty is the degree to which the retailers want the company as a supplier in the future. This meaning of loyalty measures continuity used in previous studies and could compromise both the favourable attitude and perceived or real lack of alternatives.
Blocker et al. (2011), *Journal of the Academy of Marketing Science*	The authors studied the impact of the proactive customer orientation construct on value creation by taking a novel approach that examines the proactive customer orientation → value → satisfaction → loyalty chain using data from 800 business customers in India, Singapore, Sweden, the United Kingdom and the United States.	They assess loyalty defined in terms of a customer's intent to repurchase.
Bubb and Van Rest (1973), *Industrial Marketing Management*	The authors describe a study of a market, in which perceived product quality, pressure from the ultimate consumer and loyalty affect the buying decision outcome.	Loyalty becomes the means whereby past buying decisions affect the current one, and loyalty behaviour can be recognised as a tendency for customers to repeatedly buy from a particular supplier.
Cahill, Goldsby, Knemeyer and Wallenburg (2010), *Journal of Business Logistics*	A satisfaction – loyalty model is first established and tested in the context of service relationships formed between logistics service providers (LSPs) and their customers.	The authors define customer loyalty as the intention of a buyer of logistics services to purchase the same services (retention) and additional services (expansion) from the current provider in the future, as well as the buyer's activities in recommending this provider to others (referral).

Davis-Sramek et al. (2008), *Journal of Operations Management*	The overarching goal of this research is to examine the importance to operations managers of understanding the order fulfilment needs and expectations of their retail customers and to establish the value-added role that operations management plays in developing retailer loyalty. Empirical evidence is provided on the relationships between relational order fulfilment service, operational order fulfilment Service, satisfaction, affective commitment, purchase behaviour and loyalty. The sample was collected in the independent retail segment within the consumer durable manufacturer's customer base.	Loyalty was conceptualised as the relationship between affective commitment and purchase behaviour. Purchase behaviour is defined as the likelihood of buying a manufacturer's products or services again in the future.
Daugherty, Stank and Ellinger (1998), *Journal of Business Logistics*	Reports on a survey of buyers in the personal products industry, which found vendor distribution or logistics service to significantly and positively affect customer satisfaction and customer loyalty.	Loyalty is a long-term commitment to repurchase involving both a cognitive attitude towards the selling firm and repeated patronage.
Dick and Basu (1994), *Journal of Academy Marketing Science*	Conceptual paper that discussed loyalty from different sides. Cognitive, affective and conative antecedents of relative attitude are identified as contributing to loyalty, along with motivational, perceptual and behavioural consequences. Implications for research and for the management of loyalty are derived.	Customer loyalty is viewed as the strength of the relationship between an individual's relative attitude and repeat patronage. The authors propose four conditions related to loyalty: loyalty, latent loyalty, spurious loyalty and no loyalty.
Ellinger et al. (1999), *Transportation Research Part E*	A survey of buyers in the personal products industry was used to examine three methods of listening to customers. Frequency of vendor meetings with customers, formalised contact through the solicitation of feedback and/or conducting surveys, and personal visits by senior vendor managers were found to be related to customer satisfaction, as well as customer loyalty.	Loyalty has been defined as a long-term commitment to repurchase involving both repeated patronage and a favourable attitude
Ganesh, Arnold and Reynolds (2000), *Journal of Marketing*	This research comprises two studies in which the authors examine the differences among internal customer groups in a service industry. Theory suggests and as is empirically validated here, customers who have switched service providers because of dissatisfaction seem to differ significantly from other customer groups in their satisfaction.	Customer loyalty is a combination of both commitment to the relationship and other overt loyalty behaviours.

(Continued)

Table 2.1 (Continued)

Reference	Context	Loyalty Definition
Gassenheimer, Sterling and Robicheaux (1989), *International Journal of Physical Distribution & Material Management*	An intermediary's dependency on its suppliers' marketing services is the prime reason that intermediaries establish ongoing channel relationships. To accomplish this objective, a model is developed that incorporates supplier performance and behaviour in an interactive process with dealers (distributors) in the office systems and furniture products industry.	Loyalty is meant as the intention to keep or alter the relationships between manufacturer and dealers.
Hartmann and De Grahl (2011), *Journal of Supply Chain Management*	Logistics Service Provider (LSP) flexibility is revealed as a strong driver for all the relevant aspects of loyalty, such as retention, extension and referrals, and as one of the sources of competitive advantage. A longitudinal study should investigate the linkage between LSP flexibility and loyalty, looking at the actual purchasing behaviour of the customers.	Customer loyalty was used in this study, namely through the three constructs of customer retention, customer extension and customer referrals. Customer retention measures the customer's position towards its LSP regarding repeat purchasing intentions for the same service; customer extension comprises the customer's intentions to extend the scope of the relationship by purchasing additional services from this LSP; customer referrals measure the frequency with which the LSP is recommended.
Homburg and Fürst (2005), *Journal of Marketing*	The empirical analysis is based on a dyadic data set that contains managerial assessments of companies' complaint management and complaining customers' assessments with respect to perceived justice, satisfaction and loyalty.	Customer loyalty after the complaint refers to the degree to which a customer has continued the relationship with a company after the complaint and the degree to which he or she intends to do so in the future.
Innis and La Londe (1994), *Journal of Business Logistics*	The industry of study was the auto glass aftermarket. The focus of this research was on the retailer level of the channel. A focus on the retail level of the channel allowed the effective measurement of performance levels at the wholesale level of the channel, of satisfaction with various wholesale firms and of the attitudes and purchase intentions of retailers.	Loyalty has been defined as the repeat purchase behaviour of customers.

Maignan, Ferrell and Hult (1999), *Journal of the Academy of Marketing Science*	An empirical investigation conducted in two independent samples American Marketing Association (AMA members and MBA students) examines whether components of an organisation's culture affect the level of commitment to corporate citizenship and whether corporate citizenship is conducive to business benefits.	Customer loyalty is the non-random tendency displayed by many customers to keep buying products from the same firm over time and to associate positive images with the firm's products.
Palmatier et al. (2007), *Journal of Marketing Research*	The study involved 362 buyer-salesperson dyads using triadic data (from buyer, salesperson and sales manager). The authors examine both a customer's overall loyalty to the selling firm and the customer's loyalty vested specifically in his or her salesperson.	Loyalty to the selling firm is the customer's intention to perform a diverse set of behaviours that signal a motivation to maintain a relationship with the focal firms in the B2B.
De Ruyter, Moorman and Lemmink (2001), *Industrial Marketing Management*	The results from a qualitative and quantitative study across business customers for a photocopy machine provide evidence for the influence of types of antecedents of trust, commitment and intention to stay in supplier-customer relationships in high-technology market relationships.	Loyalty indicates the customers' motivation to maintain the relationship.
Sánchez, Vijande and Gutiérrez (2011), *Industrial Marketing Management*	The main objective of this study was to examine the effects of organisational learning (OL) on satisfaction and loyalty in industrial markets. A conceptual model, in which the unit for analysis is the dyadic relationship between manufacturers and their main distributor, was proposed and tested. Specifically, increased OL in the manufacturer has a direct effect on the main distributor's degree of satisfaction and an indirect effect on his loyalty.	Loyalty is defined as the intention to carry out a varied set of behaviours that manifest the motivation to maintain the exchange relationship, such as: repeated purchase, positive WOM and price tolerance. This definition views loyalty as a combination of both behavioural (repeated purchase) and attitudinal (positive WOM and price tolerance) aspects.
Scheer, Miao and Garrett (2010), *Journal of the Academy of Marketing Science*	This research examines whether suppliers' capabilities impact Original Equipment Manufacturer (OEM) customers' dependence on the supplier and thereby generate customer loyalty. Using a sample of purchasing managers focusing on a single key component supplier, the authors examine three supplier capabilities, two dependence dimensions and three aspects of customer loyalty.	Relational loyalty is the customer firm's expressed intent to remain loyal because of its positive relationship with the supplier.

(*Continued*)

Table 2.1 (Continued)

Reference	Context	Loyalty Definition
Selnes and Gønhaug (2000), *Journal of Business Research*	In a study of 150 established buyer-seller relationships in the industrial telecommunication market, the authors found that customers' affective responses to supplier reliability were different from their responses to supplier benevolence. Supplier reliability showed a strong positive effect on satisfaction with the supplier, which subsequently increased loyalty.	Loyalty is a behavioural intention to be loyal to the supplier.
Stank, Goldsby, Vickery and Savitskie (2003), *Journal of Business Logistics*	The research examines the relationships among three dimensions of logistics service performance (operational, relational, and cost performance), customer satisfaction, customer loyalty and market share. Perceptions of customers of third-party logistics (3PL) providers are used to assess 3PL performance constructs.	Loyalty is a long-term commitment and increased repurchase behaviour because loyal customers demonstrate greater resistance to counter persuasion and negative WOM.
Stank et al. (1999), *Journal of Operations Management*	A model of service performance effects on customer satisfaction and loyalty is introduced and tested in the fast food service industry using customer perceptions of provider performance rather than relying on providers' self-reported performance indicators. The research revealed that the benefit of establishing customer relationships emerges from the enhanced insight the supplier can gain regarding customer needs and desires.	Customer loyalty is defined as a long-term commitment to repurchase involving both a favourable cognitive attitude towards the selling firm and repeated patronage.
Watson et al. (2015), *Journal Academy of Marketing Science*	The study examines the consequences of heterogeneity by empirically mapping current conceptual approaches using an item-level coding of extant loyalty research, then testing how operational and study-specific characteristics moderate the strategy $\rightarrow$ loyalty $\rightarrow$ performance process through meta-analytic techniques. Prescriptive advice based on 163 studies of customer loyalty addresses three seemingly simple but very critical questions: What is customer loyalty? How is it measured? and What actually matters when it comes to customer loyalty?	Customer loyalty is a collection of attitudes aligned with a series of purchase behaviours that systematically favour one entity over competing entities.

Wetzels, De Ruyter and Van Birgelen (1998), *Journal of Business and Industrial Marketing*	This paper identifies theoretical antecedents and consequences of commitment in relationships in a services context (customers from an office equipment firm). The results of an empirical study reveal that affective commitment is related to trust in the partner's honesty and benevolence, quality of the outcome of the service process and customer satisfaction with the service being delivered.	Loyalty is considered as commitment towards a certain brand because strong positive associations between service quality, service satisfaction and loyalty have been reported extensively in the services marketing area.
Wind (1970), *Journal of Marketing Research*	The study analyses source loyalty in electronics firms. In particular, it examines the purchase of industrial components. The buyer (purchasing department) selects a source (a manufacturer, distributor or even a machine shop within the company) to supply the needed parts specified, by brand or detailed specification, by the R&D engineer or production control manager.	Source loyalty is a function of four major sets of variables: (a) the traditional task variables such as price, quality, delivery, quantity and service; (b) the buyer's past experience; (c) the organisational variables; and (d) the factors perceived by the buyer as simplifying his or her work.

However, successful firms have realised the importance of customer loyalty and are investing significant resources towards customer retention. To explain the sources of customer loyalty better within the B2B context, researchers have introduced various antecedents and developed several models, which we present in the following pages.

The role of switching costs on customer loyalty

Switching costs represent those costs involved in changing from one supplier to another (Heide and Weiss, 1995) and have traditionally entailed both monetary and non-monetary costs (Dick and Basu, 1994). Loyalty research frequently tests the role of switching costs (Oliva, Oliver and MacMillan, 1992; Mittal and Lassar, 1998; Wagner and Friedl, 2007; Brandenburg, Govindan, Sarkis and Seuring, 2014); that is, buyers who lack any strong attachment to service providers remain in the relationship due to the perceived costs of switching (Jap and Ganesan, 2000). In a business relationship context, switching costs include factors like contractual termination fees, feeling locked into particular provider technologies, the perceived difficulty of replacing an existing provider, or the investments of time and energy to build a new relationship (Wetzels et al., 1998). When a customer is dissatisfied with products or services received, he or she would need to establish a new relationship, which would require an investment of time, effort and money. These required investments constitute a barrier to moving to other service providers. Or, for example, a customer may make transaction-specific investments in a relationship with a supplier and, over time, the customer may have developed routines and procedures for dealing with the supplier. Research has consistently positioned the concept of switching costs as a powerful mechanism for influencing customers' actions by deterring them from changing to another supplier (Klemperer, 1995) and encouraging repeat purchase behaviour (Frazier, 1983; Heide and Weiss, 1995).

Switching costs or transaction-specific investments represent a binding force that arises between two partners. With the intention of exploring whether they are made of multiple dimensions, Nielson (1996) focuses on manufacturers and distributors who take care of supplying intermediate products, such as component parts, processed intermediates or raw materials. The fact that suppliers and buyers adapt to each other, investing in switching costs, is a consequence of mutual trust. These investments are also the manifestation of a conscious decision-making or corporate strategy. Trust is associated with soft assets, and the extent of cooperation is positively related to the level of trust. A positive linkage also exists for the level of cooperation and the degree of switching cost investments, at least for the soft assets case. In the B2B market, switching costs are consequently made by two dimensions: hard assets, which refers to tangible and physical investments that are made for a specific customer, such as dedicated machineries or product modifications; and soft assets, which refers to the quality and quantity of the working relationships between individuals and the way the two sides communicate. They represent a psychological and social investment.

Establishing switching costs in the form of hard assets appears to be more effective for enhancing customer loyalty.

Switching costs will be particularly relevant given their potential in specific industries in building personal ties and relationship learning. Some scholars (Burnham, Frels and Mahajan, 2003) found that various types of switching costs influence customers' intention to stay with the current service provider. The authors found empirical support for the level and types of switching costs to explain the customer's intention better than the customer's satisfaction, even within the industries where switching costs are low.

Meanwhile, the research paper of Lin, Lo and Sung (2006) explored in depth the interactive effects of trust, switching costs and information sharing on the performance of a supply chain. The authors defined switching costs as the sum of transaction costs, learning costs, artificial switching costs and setup costs. The distribution of orders affects the average fulfilment rate. When partners share more information, there is a more centralised order distribution. The trade-off between switching costs and trust affects the level of information shared and has an impact on supply chain performance. When the order demand environment is unstable, the switching costs increase the average inventory costs; however, switching costs and information sharing may increase the average inventory costs when the order demand environment is stable. Trust reduces the average fulfilment rate and cycle time. Since the findings were based on an experiment, future research should replicate the study using real data. Switching costs can include loyalty benefits that a customer no longer enjoys when the relationship with the service provider is interrupted. In situations when transaction-specific investments have been made in a buyer-supplier relationship, customers are motivated to stay in a relationship to avoid incurring switching costs, ceteris paribus.

Lam et al. (2004) examined the mediating role of customer satisfaction on the impact of customer value and customer loyalty (this latter is meant in terms of recommend and patronage type), and explored the reciprocal effects of customer satisfaction and loyalty on each other (see Figure 2.1). Loyal buyers are willing to build lasting relationships with a view to long-term results. From this impactful study, it emerges that customer value has a positive effect on customer satisfaction. Customer satisfaction has a positive effect on customer loyalty and switching costs have a positive effect on customer loyalty. The study made another noteworthy contribution finding evidence of a direct link between B2B customer value and loyalty, and speculated that much of the variance present in B2B loyalty models could be attributed to supplier switching costs. However, in the same research the hypothesis that customer satisfaction has a stronger positive effect on customer loyalty when switching costs are high than when they are low is not supported by the research.

In contrast to mass merchandise, buyers of logistical services do not make recurrent purchase decisions, but tie themselves contractually to their LSPs for reasonably long periods of time. Consequently, switches from one service provider to another usually take place at the end of contracts and the retention

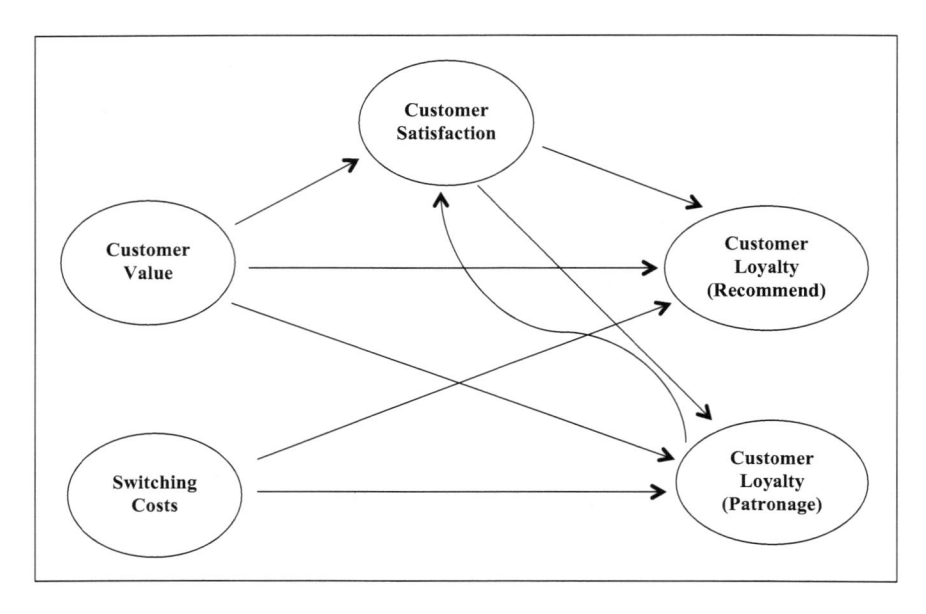

Figure 2.1 Switching costs, customer value and customer satisfaction: the impact on customer loyalty

Adapted from Lam et al. (2004)

is not determined by customer loyalty, but is created by contracts because of economic constraints (Cahill, 2006).

If consumers increase their expertise in the product line and in the industry of a certain company, switching costs, which can be psychological or financial, increase. Scholars have attempted to identify the relationship between investment expertise, perceived switching costs and customer loyalty (Bell, Auh and Smalley, 2005). The main effect of technical service quality on customer loyalty is stronger than that of functional service quality. The hypothesis that higher perceived switching costs decrease the effect of technical and functional service quality on customers' loyalty is not supported. Moreover, customers build switching costs through the development of personal relationships and the accumulation of firm-specific knowledge and sunk costs.

A study by other scholars (Whitten and Wakefield, 2006) emphasised the importance of switching costs analysis to understanding the relationships and loyalty behaviours in B2B environments. Switching costs are seen through three categories: learning costs, transaction costs and contractual costs. Switching costs is a complex and multidimensional construct and these costs are related to the difficulty of changing the established business arrangements and, consequently, improve loyalty. The information provided by the study should be tested in other service contexts and the research on switching costs should be enlarged.

Meanwhile, Merrilees and Fenech (2007) explored how purchasing agents who use the catalogue as a channel for their purchases might choose the Web as an alternative channel in the future (loyalty to a channel market). Switching costs act as a barrier and make this change more difficult. From the study, it emerged that loyalty was particularly high thanks to a history of satisfaction with repeat purchases. The reasons for choosing a Web channel were Web purchasing experience, speed and ease of use and trust of the existing catalogue retailer. Among the barriers to switching from a catalogue to a Web channel (and maybe changing supplier) were the switching costs – that is, the loss of certain benefits, such as staff contact and security.

Woisetschläger, Lentz and Evanschitzky's (2011) paper examined the effects of satisfaction and economic switching barriers, particularly their interaction with customer loyalty and WOM in the contractual service setting in the B2C context. From the study, it emerged that there are positive effects of satisfaction, economic switching barriers and social ties on customer loyalty and WOM. Moreover, economic switching barriers and social ties – both influenced by habits – interact with satisfaction. Switching barriers can be defined as social or relational switching costs or financial ones, since starting a new commercial relationship means losing benefits, and meeting setup and procedural costs. Satisfaction and economic switching costs are the most important antecedents of customer loyalty.

The role of switching costs was investigated by other scholars to understand whether they affect loyalty in a B2B relationship (Geiger et al., 2012). It appears that the value of the relationship has a stronger effect on intentions for relationship improvement, the search for alternatives and switch intention than on switching costs for both the sides of the relationship. Looking only at buyers, switching costs assume a more important role than the relationship value. Moreover, buyers build their intentions to do business in the future by looking at the current state of the relationship. It is important to underline that switching costs depend on environmental and behavioural uncertainty and on the degree of asset specificity. In Geiger et al.'s paper, switch intention is seen as the exact opposite to loyalty. Switching costs are usually assumed to alleviate a buyer's switch intentions. The hypothesis 'supplier switching costs are positively associated with its intentions for relationship enhancement' is only partly supported. Supplier switching costs are positively associated with its relational tolerance and with its tendency to search for alternatives. Buyer switching costs are negatively associated with its switch intention.

Other scholars (Heinonen et al., 2013) examined the application of the switching path analysis technique in the B2B environment. It emerges that supplier switches happen when customers perceive the inferiority of their old supplier – the so-called reactional trigger. Situational triggers also play their role: when customers change their production processes, when they change market settings and when new human resources evaluating the suppliers enter the company. Later, Park, Park and Lee (2014) investigated the effects of loyalty and switching costs towards a firm's post-adoption behaviour in using information systems. Loyalty and switching costs were shown to have a positive influence on the willingness of using an information system, with the consequence that alternatives are not evaluated.

However, B2B customers follow rational buying criteria (Verbeke, Dietz and Verwaal, 2011), typically invest more in a long-term relationship, and wish for more frequent and more customized service encounters than B2C customers. This approach leads to higher switching costs and lower customer defection rates.

Then a recent and relevant contribution from Pick and Eisend (2014) stated that market-related variables, such as alternatives and competition, have the highest influence on switching costs, reducing buyers' quality perception of a relationship and offerings. The variables that are directly related to the single seller – for example, seller investments – have a small influence on switching costs, and switching costs have a weak negative influence on switching. The effect of switching costs is higher in B2C than in B2B, while the effect on switching supplier is stronger in B2B markets than in B2C markets. Building switching costs pays off more in B2C markets compared with B2B, where they have to be prevented by other means. Such costs create a barrier in switching to other providers; thus, research on service failure and service recovery is urgently needed in future studies. Blut, Beatty, Evanschitzky and Brock (2014) distinguished between internal switching costs (i.e., costs primarily rooted in an individual customer's expertise, skills and the ability required to consider a switch) and external switching costs (i.e., the benefits offered by providers to encourage customers to stay).

Focusing on logistics outsourcing, another study focused on dependence, relationship commitment and service quality (Shong-lee Ivan Su, Huo, Liu, Kang and Zhao, 2015). Normative relationship commitment is necessary when users perceive switch dependence. Normative relationship commitment, which is developed when switching costs are perceived, also appears to be more important than instrumental relationship commitment in facilitating the adoption of 3PL logistics outsourcing. Switching providers is costly because of the switching costs related to the strategic relationship with a 3PL provider and to increased uncertainty. Switch dependence is a key driver of customised and advanced outsourcing for 3PL users in China. Researchers should take into consideration other relational factors to describe 3PL relationship management better.

To increase loyalty and retain customers in B2B settings, many companies try to build up switching barriers, thereby increasing the switching costs. The switching experience influences customer satisfaction and loyalty willingness in a negative way. Financial and relational switching costs also partially mediate customer satisfaction and loyalty. According to Matzler, Strobl, Thurner and Füller (2015), the customers that are taken from competitors may be the least loyal. In fact, customers who have experienced different switching alternatives are difficult to satisfy and low satisfaction decreases the perception of switching costs and, ultimately, loyalty. Future research should include a more comprehensive conceptualisation of switching costs with the intention of better understanding the relationship between loyalty, satisfaction and switching costs.

Customer loyalty can be high even if satisfaction, customer value and perceived switching costs are absent. As a response, other scholars have examined this thoroughly (Russo, Confente, Gligor and Autry, 2016), showing, for example, that if switching costs are high, customers are loyal even if the product return policy is not satisfactory. It is also worth noting that Russo et al.'s paper is the first to state that in the B2B sector, when different variables are considered at the same time, their impact on customer loyalty can change. Future studies might consider other combinations of attributes, such as habit and lack of motivation, to see how they affect customer loyalty. Russo et al. used a qualitative comparative analysis which assumed that the influence of attributes on a specific outcome (customer loyalty in a B2B context) depends on how the attributes are combined; this approach provides understanding of the complex phenomenon. Although the extant literature helps identify various predictors of customer loyalty, past studies have concentrated exclusively on the 'net effects' of these antecedents. Yet, there are theoretical reasons to suggest that these effects may be more complicated than they first appear. The same authors show how, according to complexity theory, real-world relationships between variables can be non-linear with abrupt switches occurring; thus, the same 'cause' can, in specific circumstances, produce different 'effects' in the context of supplier–buyer relationships.

For Blut, Evanschitzky, Backhaus, Rudd and Marck (2016) little is known about the impacts of switching costs in B2B markets, that is, on industrial markets and buyer-seller relationships. Switching costs in the B2B context includes procedural costs (setup costs, behavioural and cognitive costs, and evaluation costs), financial costs (sunk costs and lost performance costs, i.e., benefits that are lost with the switching) and relational switching costs (personal relationship loss costs and brand relationship loss costs). The relational switching costs are the more important for guaranteeing customer loyalty. A longitudinal research should be conducted – to generalise the results, similar investigations about other sectors and countries are necessary.

In addition, consistent with the interdisciplinary focus of our book, we draw attention to the need for future research to investigate additional constructs outside the traditional domain of marketing (e.g., SCM, organisational behaviour, production economics) that might help theory development within the B2B customer loyalty area. For example, considering the dynamic environments in which most firms operate, it would be interesting to examine the role of supply chain agility and innovation. Finally, a qualitative approach would help provide better understanding and uncover additional factors that affect customer loyalty. Also, lack of motivation or acting out of habit can allow a company to experience customer loyalty, even though other satisfactions are not experienced; that is another field for more research.

Therefore, firms in the supply chain may form different kinds of exchange relationships with supply chain members. For managers, this means, for example, that when customers have low defection barriers (low switching costs), they should closely monitor and attempt to increase the customers' level of satisfaction to ensure customers stay loyal.

Linking customer satisfaction and customer loyalty

Customer satisfaction and its measurements have been widely studied, though no general, universally accepted definition exists, mainly because there are different visions of the concept, such as those linked to a single or to cumulative transactions. Furthermore, customer satisfaction and service quality are related concepts that sometimes appear synonymous, especially to practitioners, though empirical research mostly affirms that they are different concepts. If service performance goes beyond expectations, the customer is highly satisfied or even delighted.

An efficient physical distribution is a possible method through which customer service is realised. According to Innis and La Londe (1994), customer service represents the key to achieving customer satisfaction and loyalty. Customer service has a strong and positive effect on customer satisfaction, cognitive attitudes and repurchase intentions as loyalty. Customer service can thus be used to obtain a competitive advantage, increase the market share and enhance loyalty. It is often considered a key goal of SCM; however, only if service offerings create value for customers will they lead to behaviours that improve performance.

The construct of customer satisfaction has been widely explored in the last decades. Nevertheless, it is not immediately possible to identify a generally accepted definition, partly because there are different visions of the concept: one linked to the single transaction, and the other associated with cumulative transactions. While the former is viewed as a post-choice evaluative judgement of a specific purchase occasion, the latter describes satisfaction that accumulates across a series of encounters and is a more fundamental indicator of a supplier's overall performance through time (Lambert and Harrington, 1989; Oliva et al., 1992; Rust and Zahorik, 1993; Anderson et al., 1994). Satisfaction is usually defined as the difference between performance expectations, specifically referring to a good or service, and experience-based perceived performance. It is well known that customer satisfaction is positively related to desired organisational outcomes such as loyalty (Fornell, 1992), and a more dominant view shows satisfaction as a judgement based on the cumulative experience with a specific product and service (Anderson et al., 1994); building interdependent or closer relationships with customers is thought to increase customer satisfaction (Parasuraman, Berry and Zeithaml, 1991) and to correlate with customer retention (Fornell, 1992).

Thus, in recent decades, customer satisfaction has become a central construct in marketing and has been linked to customer loyalty and the prices customers are willing to pay for a service or product (Homburg, Koschate and Hoyer, 2005). Moreover, firms view customer satisfaction as a strategic imperative and make significant investments to ensure customer satisfaction. In B2B settings, satisfaction is 'a positive affective state resulting from the appraisal of all aspects of a firm's working relationship with another firm' (Anderson and Narus, 1984, p. 66). However, satisfaction and loyalty should not be viewed as surrogates for one another; in the following discussion, we present some, but not all, of the different perspectives of linking satisfaction with loyalty in a supply chain context.

For instance, the study conducted by Daugherty, Ellinger and Plair (1997) concerned the relationship between the retail industry and the selling firms. The link between customer satisfaction and customer loyalty was already evident from previous research. It was found that key account strategic service initiatives may positively influence both customer satisfaction and customer loyalty. Key account buyers reported higher levels of customer satisfaction, repurchase intentions and relationship commitment than buyers for accounts receiving regular and standardised service. Moreover, some empirical evidence was given by Stank et al. (1999), who indicated that there is a strong link between relational performance and satisfaction. Meanwhile, the logistics field describes how order fulfilment creates customer satisfaction through the 'seven R's' – a firm's ability to deliver the right amount of the right product at the right place at the right time in the right condition at the right price with the right information (Stock and Lambert, 2001).

Focusing on industrial services and the fast food industry, some scholars have investigated the relationship between operational and relational performance on customer satisfaction and loyalty (Stank et al., 2003). The attention is on the perceptions about providers seen from the perspective of customers. It emerges that operational and relational performances affect customer satisfaction and consequently customer loyalty. Therefore, those service providers who can excel in their operations and who build strong relationships with their customers reach higher levels of customer loyalty and satisfaction. Creating customised solutions contributes to higher levels of loyalty and, at the same time, this can reduce the supply chain risk for competitors in the relationship (Borghesi and Gaudenzi, 2012).

Homburg and Stock (2005) investigated the link between salespeople's job satisfaction and customer satisfaction. They found that the link exists and it includes a positive relationship between the two constructs. It is particularly evident when the two sides often interact, when customer integration in the value-creating process is intense and when the company deals with innovative products or services. Future research could continue to investigate the B2B setting to show the high relevance of salespeople as key to building a lasting bond based on loyalty.

Research about loyalty in the B2B industry is generally known as relationship marketing or service quality research. The paper of Chiou and Droge (2006) focuses on loyalty in high-involvement and high-service luxury product markets. Companies can increase loyalty by building a trustworthy image and creating exchange-specific assets. Overall satisfaction is an antecedent of loyalty. Moreover, consumers meet different costs in reducing adverse selection problems with information and, for these reasons, the negative effect of product-market expertise on loyalty must be considered. Trust and consumer satisfaction are the basis for behavioural loyalty. Marketers should invest in consumer satisfaction and in ad hoc marketing programmes that can encourage consumers to make Specific Asset Investments (SAIs) (SAIs also include switching costs). The study relies on a framework that was designed for B2B contexts, but it includes a study in the B2C industry.

Naumann, Williams and Khan (2009) set some propositions with the aim of better predicting how loyalty is built. They conducted research thanks to the participation of a Fortune 100 company active in different business units and in the B2B environment. The authors proposed that customers acquired after a merger or acquisition will show lower levels of customer loyalty. Likewise, those customers that choose the company when prices are set low for a promotion are less loyal, while customers with an increasing market share tend to be more loyal compared with those who have a decreasing market share. Further, customers who operate in a healthy and growing context are supposed to be more loyal than those who operate in a shrinking one. Lastly, customer organisations that have a frequent change of executives or supply chain leadership are less loyal. According to these findings, the link between customer satisfaction and loyalty should not be taken for granted. It appears that satisfied customers would recommend their supplier or their service provider because they are satisfied, but they often switch them for other reasons, including a better price. For these reasons, the authors contend that traditional customer satisfaction research will never be able to predict customer loyalty.

Other scholars have focused on environmental stewardship and included sustainability issues, relying on the B2B setting of consumer services and contact centre services (De Ruyter, De Jong and Wetzels, 2009). Stewardship (being green) relates positively to customer perceptions but not to sales performance. Past customer satisfaction ratings have a positive impact on environmental stewardship and this may happen because the role of stewards is to act in the service of the stakeholders' interests. To generalise the findings, additional research about the B2B context is suggested.

Client loyalty in the B2B e-marketplace has not been investigated deeply. Some scholars (Janita and Miranda, 2013) aimed to fill this research gap, focusing on the role of image, quality, satisfaction and value in loyalty. From the analysis, it emerges that satisfaction does not generate any direct effect on client loyalty. Conversely, the image of the e-marketplace and user-perceived quality and value are drivers of customer loyalty. The findings of Janita and Miranda are relevant because the paper was the first to investigate the determinants of loyalty in a B2B e-marketplace. Perceived quality is the most important factor in gaining user loyalty. However, the e-marketplace image also plays a relevant role in building loyalty and a lasting relationship.

From a logistics perspective, customer satisfaction is defined as the result of a cognitive and affective evaluation, based on total purchase and consumption experience with the logistics service over time. Some comparison standards are compared to the actually perceived performance (Davis-Sramek et al., 2008).

In this case, when satisfaction rises above a certain threshold, or the trust zone, purchase behaviour climbs rapidly. Meanwhile, when satisfaction falls below the lower threshold, or the defection zone, purchase behaviour declines rapidly. This implies that satisfaction must be high enough to encourage behavioural loyalty, or low enough to diminish it. However, in the context of the order fulfilment service quality dimension, the authors found that satisfaction leads to affective commitment and this emotional attachment is what influences a customer's subsequent purchase behaviour.

Generally managers seemed surprised to find that customer satisfaction is not just about supplying quality goods and services at the right price or developing marketing initiatives that have differentiated features with respect to competitors. In other words, customer satisfaction is not enough to create long-lasting relationships. Becoming a preferred supplier in any industry today inevitably means that a high priority must be placed on delivering superior customer service to keep the customers connected with the company.

Customer value and its impact on customer loyalty

When assessing factors that impact customer loyalty, it is important to account for customer value. Customer value means, in brief, the trade-off between benefits and sacrifices that stem from a provider's product and relationship resources, which customers consider are facilitating their goals. Value creation is a central concept in the management and organisation literature, both at the micro level (individual, group) and the macro level (organisational theory, strategic management) (Lepak, Smith and Taylor, 2007). As the name implies, 'customer value theory emphasises the importance of being customer-focused and aligning resources and capabilities for superior value creation' (Slater, 1997, p. 164). Until now, research on building customer value theory in B2B contexts has focused on defining the concept (Flint, Woodruff and Gardial, 1997), measuring its antecedents (Ulaga and Eggert, 2006b), exploring value creation as a process (Grönroos and Ravald, 2011) that dynamically unfolds in relationships (Blocker and Flint, 2007) or studying how the customers' values change (Flint and Mentzer, 2000) or understanding how internal integration can create value by eliminating redundancies, creating efficiencies and reducing costs (Mollenkopf, Frankel and Russo, 2011).

Customer value as buyer behaviour has been researched for approximately 25 years. These studies cover the consumer (Holbrook, 1994; Smith and Colgate, 2007) and business contexts (Anderson and Narus, 1984; Lapierre, 2000; Ulaga, 2003; Anderson, Narus and Van Rossum, 2006; Ritter and Walter, 2012). Perceived value notion, which is broader than that of perceived quality, on the benefits side lists attributes such as technical, delivery time, functional quality, design and innovation. The total sacrifices perceived by the buyer are listed as price, time, effort, transportation costs, communication cost, installation, repairs, maintenance and cost of ownership (Ulaga and Eggert, 2006a; Corsaro and Snehota, 2010).

The importance of customer value is significant, especially in the B2B context where the supply base is more concentrated, and firms need to retain key customers to be profitable in the long term. In particular, the literature of this field has emphasised the supplier-buyer relationship and the extension of customer orientation and value creation to the whole supply chain. As a consequence, according to relationship marketing, the value perceived by the customer in a supplier-buyer relationship (called total episode value) is the result of a trade-off between benefits and sacrifices of both the single episode and the relationship as a whole.

In the service-dominant context of industrial complexity, intermediaries provide a combination of goods and services to address problems faced by the buyer firm. Understanding the value perceived by different players in the marketing channel is critical to the success of delivering customer value throughout the chain to the end consumer (Grönroos and Voima, 2013). This is also important from a managerial perspective (the supplier) to provide a better understanding of perceived value from the perspective of the critical role of this player. Even if in B2B 'value' has many interpretations (Lindgreen, Hingley, Grant and Morgan, 2012), in this book customer value is considered to be the trade-off between benefits and sacrifices that stem from a provider's product and service offerings.

Substantial evidence suggests that customer value is positively related to customer loyalty (Tsai, Tsai and Chang, 2010; Blocker et al., 2011; Janita and Miranda, 2013). Understanding the value chain from the customers' perspective is relevant in identifying customers' unexpressed and latent needs and potential loyalty drivers. Customers may stay loyal to a supplier if they feel they are receiving greater value than the value they would obtain from the supplier's competitors.

Given the significant effect of customer value on customer loyalty, it is possible that when customers' perceptions of value are high the relationship between switching costs and customer loyalty is strengthened. Moreover, it is possible that customer value perceptions can bypass satisfaction feelings and lead directly to loyalty behaviour. However, recent evidence validates a direct link between customer value and satisfaction and suggests that a more significant relationship between customer value and loyalty is mediated by satisfaction (Lam et al., 2004). This means that customer satisfaction mediates totally the relationship between customer value and customer loyalty, in the sense that the greater the customer value, the greater the customer satisfaction and customer loyalty.

Thus, by investigating the role of customer value change in business relationships in a multi-market context, a contribution is made both to an emerging theory of business customer value change and to managers as they look for insights to build a base of loyal customers amidst rapidly changing markets (Flint, Blocker and Boutin, 2011). Understanding customer value, anticipating when this value changes, and making it easy for customers to receive that value and buy our products and services is not always easy to achieve, but it is essential for maintaining customers and growing market share. Scholars maintain high interest in exploring how customer value contributes to key relationship performance indicators like satisfaction and loyalty. Value creation is concerned with issues such as what drives customer value and why, tracking how customer value is changing, and understanding customers' satisfaction levels and degrees of loyalty.

Managers and scholars have shown a dominant interest in aggregate perceptions of value as indicators of other important phenomena like customer satisfaction and loyalty. However, increasingly in today's business markets, buyers and suppliers are developing close collaborative relationships to provide opportunities to meet the pressure of competition and to achieve superior rewards. In fact, there is a need for suppliers to compete proactively in the market through the anticipation of what their customers might need in the future. As such, a recent evolution of customer value into so-called customer value anticipation (CVA) has occurred. This proactive approach is not easy to pursue because of the lack of knowledge about the behaviours and activities that suppliers can adopt. Consequently, one of the key elements of CVA is the skill for the firm to develop a set of behaviours known as 'proactive market orientation', in which a business attempts to discover, understand and satisfy the latent needs of customers through delivering greater value. In relation to this, there are several gaps in the literature on the role of value anticipation and on the role the supplier plays in contributing to the level of value that customers perceive suppliers help to create. This is particularly so in different business contexts and in industry competition. In detail, CVA refers to

> A supplier's ability to look ahead at what specific customers will value from supplier relationships including their product and service offerings and the benefits they create given the monetary and non-monetary sacrifices that must be made to obtain those offering benefits.
>
> (Flint et al., 2011, p. 1)

Flint and colleagues provide a new framework with the link between this dimension and the perception of customer satisfaction and loyalty from a customer's perspective, in the sense that suppliers have been evaluated for their overall ability to anticipate customers' needs and have processes that anticipate value (Flint et al., 2011).

For managers it is relevant to understand how value creation is highly dependent on the capacity of the focal company to combine the goal of suppliers and customers within the inter-functional relationships between operations, logistics, marketing, procurement and planning. Cross-functional integration refers to a process of interdepartmental interaction and collaboration in which multiple functions work together in a cooperative manner to arrive at mutually acceptable outcomes for their organisation. Consistent delivery of value is the foundation of effective, trusting, relationships between functions in the supply chain. Cross-functional integration is an internal premise to generate the ability in the company to be able to deliver value, even to anticipate customer value. This is especially true as product and service offerings themselves become more and more complicated to differentiate within highly competitive industry settings; therefore, the absence of perceived value would affect customer loyalty.

We encourage future research that would unpack the complex interactions between value (or anticipation) and satisfaction loyalty costs to understand better the case of a firm that can experience high customer loyalty in the absence of satisfaction and customer value. For instance, customers' lack of motivation to find new suppliers is a dangerous scenario that companies should take into consideration. Future research can investigate more about this.

Logistics service quality (LSQ) and its impact on customer loyalty

A growing stream of supply chain and logistics literature has highlighted the importance of understanding logistics service from the perspective of the customer (Mentzer, Flint and Hult, 2001; Stank et al., 2003). These studies used the service quality literature to develop measures that capture the perceptions of customers on logistics service attributes. Originally, service quality is a measure of how well the service delivered matches customer expectations, and delivering service quality means conforming to customer expectations on a consistent basis (Lewis and Booms, 1983). One of the key dyadic relationships across the supply chain is between the logistics service provider and the manufacturer. Over time, the concept of the logistics service provider has developed towards a service offering of greater complexity, combining new added-value services that are often involved in the strategic coordination of customers' supply chain activities. Some customers may require one level of service to remain loyal, while others may not expect or need that same level of service or attributes. Taken as a whole, logistics customer service influences several important outcomes, including customer satisfaction and loyalty and operational and financial performance (Lambert and Harrington, 1989;Daugherty et al., 1997;Leuschner, Carter, Goldsby and Rogers, 2014).

A key role in the modern-day supply chain is linked to the role of 3PL. A clearer understanding of the drivers of logistics outsourcing performance could help manage these interfaces, and might be achieved through more empirical research. We focus the following paragraphs on 3PL and the importance of LSQ for the customer.

Logistics management helps determine customer satisfaction across the supply chain, particularly in relation to 3PL services. In the logistics discipline, customer service has two aspects: the first involves cycle time, on-time delivery and inventory availability, while the second involves responsiveness, which is any handling of individual customer requests beyond traditional service measures (Davis and Mentzer, 2006).

The rich research tradition dedicated to service quality and customer satisfaction with logistics centres mostly on service quality in supplier-buyer relationships, and to a lesser extent on 3PL relationships. To enhance their competitiveness, many companies outsource some activities, which enables them to improve their operational efficiency, reduce costs, focus more on their core competencies and improve their innovation capabilities. Outsourcing thus spans multiple business functions, such as information technology management, service, logistics, manufacturing, financial services and human resource management. Companies use their logistics network to deliver products to their customers, and therefore it can significantly impact firm performance. As such, logistics customer service is the output of a firm's logistics system.

Competition in logistics service outsourcing is high, and the paper of Hartmann and de Grahl (2011, p. 35) focused on the role of flexibility of the Logistics Service Provider (LSP) as a possible key factor to build competitive advantage. LSP flexibility was found to be a strong driver for all the relevant aspects of loyalty, such as retention, extension and referrals, and to be one of the sources of competitive advantage. Collaboration influences flexibility and customer loyalty in a positive way.

Mentzer et al. (2001) and Rafiq and Jaafar (2007) studied different LSQ dimensions, mostly related to the order placement process (information quality, personal contact quality and ordering procedures) and order distribution process (order condition, timeliness, order discrepancy and order accuracy) and their impact on satisfaction. These logistics service mechanisms differ from the more general framework of service quality already studied in marketing research (Parasuraman et al., 1991).

Stank et al. (2003) suggested that two dimensions of service performance – operational and relational – are relevant in an industrial service context. Rafele condensed these indicators to three logistics quality dimensions: tangible components, fulfilment methods and informative actions. Flint, Larsson, Gammelgaard and Mentzer (2005) showed emerging innovation aspects of logistics customer service. Other scholars (Davis and Mentzer, 2006) used qualitative evidence to explore how perceptions of LSQ affect loyalty in supplier–customer relationships.

Some scholars attempted to evaluate a possible increase in customers' perceptions of product or service quality, looking at the impacts and improvements on relationship quality and customer loyalty (Chumpitaz Caceres and Paparoidamis, 2007). The authors stated that relationship satisfaction has a strong and significant effect on trust, commitment and loyalty. When customers are satisfied with the relationship with the advertising firm, business loyalty reaches higher levels. Relationship commitment, seen as the involvement between the two sides, brings positive effects on loyalty as well – loyalty increases thanks to trust. Moreover, higher levels of customer satisfaction with the relationship cause higher levels of commitment and trust in the relationship. Relationship satisfaction is a mediator between the dimensions of service quality (advertising and commercial service) and trust, commitment and loyalty. Internal and external service quality initiatives carry through to supplier's loyalty and satisfaction. Service quality is in fact related to loyalty, satisfaction, competitive advantage and organisational performance.

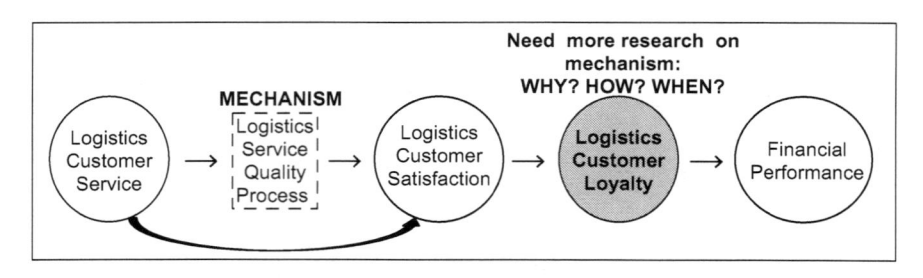

Figure 2.2 The evolution of Logistics Customer Service (LCS)
Adapted by Stank et al. (2017)

Davis-Sramek et al. (2008) investigated the importance of order fulfilment expectations by looking at the relationship between manufacturers and retailers. In the establishment of scales, loyalty is a mediator between customer satisfaction and firm performance. The study revealed that operations management has a strategic relevance for the manufacturer. How the customer perceives the order fulfilment service determines satisfaction building and retailer loyalty and, consequently, a competitive advantage. Loyalty has emotional and behavioural elements that must be seen together, since they represent a causal relationship between affective commitment and purchase behaviour. According to Large, Kramer and Hartmann (2011), when 3PL providers adapt to customers' requests, loyalty and the stability of the B2B relationship are better off.

Recently, Thai (2013) revealed how a full picture of LSQ could be analysed to understand the most critical aspects to enhance perceived LSQ. Meanwhile, Leuschner et al. (2014) provided evidence that logistics customer service has a significant positive relationship with firm performance and that LSQ can indeed be a source of competitive advantage.

Further, a recent study by Stank, Pellathy, Mollenkopf and Bell (2017) demonstrated more specifically how different elements of middle-range theorising could be applied in the case of logistics customer service. Further research needs to explore mechanisms and contexts related to why, how and when customer satisfaction leads to logistics customer loyalty and then to firm performance (see Figure 2.2).

Understanding logistics from the customer's perspective can enhance the service offerings and be a tool for differentiation and for satisfaction. Then firms can focus on those elements of service that will have the greatest impact on influencing attitudinal and behavioural loyalty. Further, it is important for managers to understand what drives customers to keep and develop the relationship in the B2B context. If the loyalty concept can be better understood, then managers will have more clarity about what level of logistics service to provide to different customer groups, optimising the limited resources they have.

Trust, commitment and customer loyalty

According to Morgan and Hunt (1994), commitment and trust are key mediating variables between five antecedents (relationship termination costs, relationship benefits, shared values, communication and opportunistic behaviour) and five relationship outcomes (acquiescence, propensity to leave, cooperation, functional conflict and decision-making uncertainty). Relationship marketing researchers agree that commitment and trust are key variables which facilitate the establishment of long collaboration (and loyalty customer). Moreover, relationships marketing enables trusting and committed relationships between supply chain members. According to Gundlach et al. (1995, p. 1), commitment is 'an essential part of successful long-term relationships'; it has also been defined as 'an implicit or explicit pledge of relational continuity between exchange partners' (Dwyer et al., 1987, p. 19). Other scholars have argued that committed partners are willing to make relationship-specific investments because they are confident about the longevity of the relationship (Anderson and Weitz, 1992). There are several impacts of trust and commitment on cooperation; thus, trust works to overcome mutual difficulties such as power, conflict and low profitability (Dwyer et al., 1987).

Previous studies using business samples found that affective commitment and trust in benevolence strongly influence the intention to continue the relationship (Wetzels et al., 1998). The literature has often stated that a relationship between trust and commitment exists but few studies in the supply chain and logistics context have investigated it. Meanwhile, from the study of Kwon and Suh (2004), it emerges that trust towards a supply chain partner is positively related to specific investments the two sides have made and negatively related to behavioural uncertainty. These specific investments are investments in physical and human capital that are addressed to a specific partner. Switching costs appear if the relationship should end. If a supply chain partner has a good reputation, trust is easily built in the relationship. Moreover, the degree of loyalty is strongly connected with the level of trust.

Cooperation, communication, trust and adaptation to expectations explain satisfaction, according to Cambra-Fierro and Polo-Redondo (2008). To guarantee loyalty, suppliers should identify the real needs of their customers, managing cooperation, communication and trust. However, generalisation of the results of this study is not possible because it concerns the Spanish environment only.

For example, some scholars (Wallenburg et al., 2011) examined how loyalty is built considering commitment and trust, comparing Germany and the United States. The research considered the outsourcing relationships between firms and their LSP. Commitment and trust were revealed to be strong drivers of retention and referrals. Commitment was also a strong predictor of loyalty: building long-term relationships with LSPs based on trust is the key to promoting loyalty. In relation to the United States, trust had no direct effect on retention while commitment had a strong and direct link with loyalty. In relation to Germany, however, trust had a stronger relationship with loyalty. Even if the American and the German contexts appear similar at a first glance, culture plays its role: trust in Germany is a direct antecedent of loyalty, while in the United States it assumes a sort of relevance only if commitment is built between the sides.

With the aim of increasing customer loyalty in the B2B industry, managers should look at value and relationship equity rather than brand equity. Customer equity, that is, the value that a customer attributes to the selling firm, must be understood through its triple meaning. According to Ramaseshan, Rabbanee and Hsin Hui (2013, p. 54), brand equity refers to the importance of the corporate brand – it is high when customers think that the brand is unique and desirable. Value equity considers the evaluation of products by looking at their utility. Relationship value depends on the relationships that are built among the B2B partners and observing how customers are familiar with the employees of the selling company. If relationship value is present, customers tend to purchase continuously in the future.

The role of managing returns on customer loyalty

The concepts of reverse logistics and returns management have evolved over the years, passing through different stages and becoming more popular today; however, they are often the forgotten stepchild of business management and strategy. Returns offer a means for companies to create value through improved cost management, increased revenue and improved customer relationships after several days.

The story of returns began with Montgomery Ward – an American furniture shop established in 1892. It was the first to offer a 100% guarantee to customers, providing a full refund if the customer was not satisfied with the product he or she had bought. To our knowledge, it is here that we find the roots of customer return policies.[1] However, in 1934 Brock pointed out how 'a more wholesome relations between buyer and seller, better retail merchandising, and even a reduction in style waste' might reduce the loss for manufacturer in managing returns.

For a comprehensive overview of reverse logistics and returns management, we primarily refer the reader to Rubio, Chamorro and Miranda's (2008) extensive analysis of the evolution of reverse flow research. For more recent developments in this field, we refer the reader to latest reviews by Govindan, Soleimani and Kannan (2015) and Rogers, Melamed and Lembke (2012) because they are the most comprehensive studies in this research stream.

To understand better the factors affecting customer loyalty, we investigated the role of product returns, previously studied in B2C online and offline contexts (Mollenkopf, Rabinovich, Laseter and Boyer, 2007; Petersen and Kumar, 2009; Walsh, Albrecht, Kunz and Hofacker, 2016). Petersen, Anderson, Kumar and Shah (2015) found that in the B2C context a company can increase its short- and long-term profits if it can account for the perceived risk related to product returns and if it manages the related costs. However, customers in the B2B context may return products for a variety of reasons, including in-transit damage, expired date code, product discontinuation or replacement, product off-season, retailer's high inventory and product defects (Rogers et al., 2012).

Pollock (2007) stated that returns management is a useful tool to improve customer satisfaction. The best-selling companies are those that can give to their customers exactly what they expect to have and create and maintain a competitive advantage. The purpose of the firm should be to keep the customer so content (before, during and following the purchase) that he or she will remain loyal in the future and repurchase the products from the same supplier. Firms that integrate new technologies into their services are those that are usually able to establish a stronger customer relationship.

Further, customers are also affected by a supplier's product and packaging quality. These problems make selling the product difficult for retailer (i.e., loss of consumer purchases, unsatisfied consumer and/or store loyalty) and can lead to shrinking retailer sales and/or margins (Mollenkopf et al., 2011). The main characteristics of B2B returns are that the returns time is fixed, the returns quantity is much larger and of higher value and the returns quality is generally the same as that of new products (Li, Wei and Cai, 2012). Huang, Yang and Wong (2016) discussed the importance for future research to address outcomes, not just antecedents, of supply chain structures that focus on unique capabilities in managing returns in the B2B context.

In addition, managing the flow of returned products is becoming more important to the success of firms' supply chains because of the high volumes of returned products, their value to customers and the signalling effects of quality that such programmes elicit (Petersen and Kumar, 2009; Bower and Maxham, 2012; Hazen, Overstreet, Hall, Huscroft and Hanna, 2015). Managing product returns involves significant operational challenges and high costs; however, product returns also present an opportunity to manage customer relationships and strengthen customer loyalty (Mollenkopf et al., 2007). For instance, returns could be viewed as a service recovery opportunity. Recovery responsiveness relates to how effectively the company handles problems and returns; in managing returns, suppliers have the opportunity to resolve complaints from customers unsatisfied with their initial supply experiences and ensure that these customers transition from unsatisfied to satisfied. Conversely, bad product return experience can contribute to switching behaviour and negatively impact customer loyalty (Askariazad and Babakhani, 2015). Craighead, Karwan and Miller (2004) found that loyal customers in the context of service recovery are most likely to suffer a decline in loyalty when problems are not resolved. As such, researchers have highlighted the need for additional research on this topic within the B2B context. A key premise of the current book is that a robust returns management process could help increase customer loyalty by overcoming switching behaviour, poor customer service and complaints.

In fact, a survey conducted by Deloitte and Arvato in 2013 revealed that returns management strongly influences the supply chain and that it represents a significant portion of the costs sustained; more precisely, compared with the cost of goods sold, an average of between 7% and 10% is given by reverse logistics. The return rate in e-commerce is between 10% and 30% for many different categories of products that impact sooner or later on the manufacturer.

The product return rate in the traditional retailing industry is more than 8% (National Retail Federation, 2015). In some industries, the cost of processing product returns can range from somewhere between $6 and $18 per item (Roenisch, 2013). The importance of this topic has caught the attention of practitioners as well as academics. This increased attention has reinforced the emergence of reverse supply chain operations management as a key strategic capability for any organisation within the supply chain (Greve and Davis, 2012; Hazen, Hall and Hanna, 2012).

Manufacturers are becoming more interested in the reverse supply chain capabilities of their LSPs (Langley and Capgemini, 2015). The effective execution of reverse supply chain operations is gradually being given strategic consideration. This strategic importance is highlighted by the recent acquisition of GENCO (a recognised third-party leader in returns management) by FedEx (Black, 2014). LSPs have become an integral part in managing reverse supply chain operations across a multitude of different industries.

Returns can often be perceived as a business conundrum: on the marketing side, returns policies are part of the sales assurance process – promising liberal returns allowances reduces the purchase risk for the buyer, and thus enhances sales. But on the operations side, liberal returns policies mean more returns, more processing and, thus, more expenses incurred (Mollenkopf et al., 2016). Consequently, efficiency is the key to control costs. But efficient operations are not sufficient. Broader SCM issues also come into play as the entire reverse channel is evaluated and rethought. While returns have often been considered

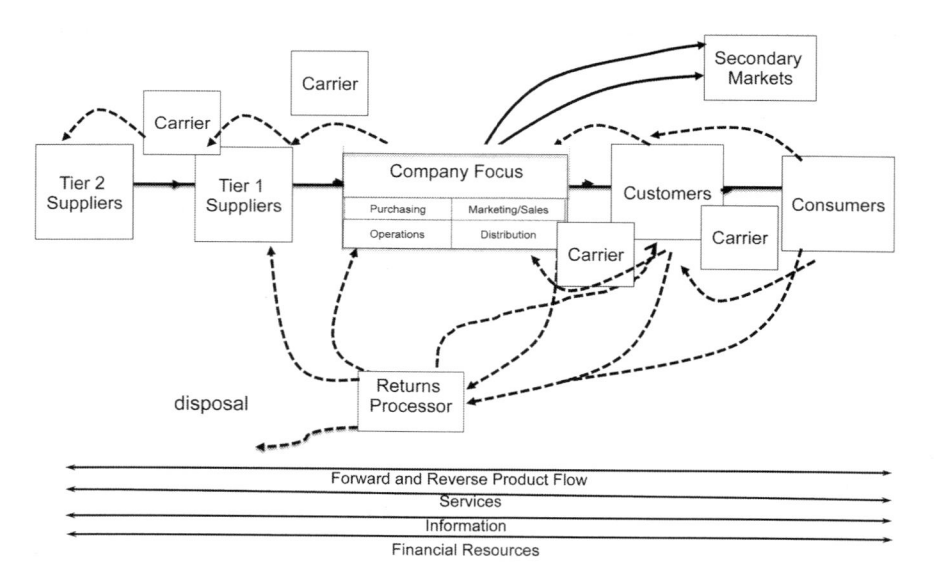

Figure 2.3 The integrated forward/reverse supply chain

Adapted from Mollenkopf, Frankel and Russo (2016)

the ugly stepchild of SCM, or a 'necessary evil' of doing business, we contend that such a view is short-sighted (Petersen et al., 2015). More recently Russo, Confente, Gligor and Cobelli (2017) reveal the complex relationship between returns management and repeated purchase intent. Specifically, their results indicate that the effect of product returns on repurchase intent and customer loyalty is opposite to the effect of customer value, depending on the value of customer value.

Poorly managed returns processes can indeed be a drain on a firm's profitability, but well-managed, strategically focused returns programmes may provide an opportunity for managers to create value – for their companies, for their supply chain partners and even for the ultimate consumer. Given how other sectors have tended to mimic the retail behaviour of selling, it is likely that such returns will become commonplace across industries. From the customers' perspective, a reliable and quick returns management service has become an important component of the service bundle and a hallmark of high service quality that ensures customer loyalty. As a manager said to us recently:

> Even if the volume of returns is not substantial for us, the work of the customer service is fundamental because it is directly in contact with the customers; therefore, its contribution is fundamental to gain customers' loyalty and to ensure the firm's profit.

Returns are often linked to an increase in operational costs terms, but rarely thought of as a means to enhance the supplying firm's competitiveness in its market environment. Otherwise, the implications of poorly managed returns are also recognised and understood in terms of a decrease in customer repurchase intent or in a damage of brand perception.

Customer loyalty and word of mouth (WOM)

WOM can be defined as 'an oral, person-to-person communication between a receiver and a communicator whom the receiver perceives as non-commercial, regarding a brand, product, or service' (Arndt, 1967, p. 3). Traditional WOM has been shown to play a major role in customers' buying decisions.

In fact, included in the conceptualisation of loyalty by Palmatier et al. (2007), beyond the intention to repeat purchasing, WOM has been considered a dimension of customer loyalty. Consequently, profits from WOM referrals are considered one of the most important reasons to strive for a long-term relationship with customers (von Wangenheim and Bayón, 2004). Although loyal customers may not necessarily purchase the product again, they may provide positive WOM reviews.

It seems reasonable to argue that customer acquisition through referrals is an important goal for companies, not only because of the reduced costs of acquisitions, but also because clients gained through referrals are easier to satisfy and retain. In particular, a loyal customer will recommend your company to someone else – becoming an unpaid advocate of your business – and WOM is the most effective, least expensive form of marketing (Hart and Johnson, 1999; Molinari, Abratt and Dion, 2008).

Historically, the term 'word of mouth' was used to describe interactions (mostly verbal) among customers. But with the advent of Internet, individuals can interact with other people in numerous ways that were unavailable in the past, ranging from social networking sites, blogs, wikis, recommendation sites and online communities (Hennig-Thurau et al., 2010). Consequently, the potential impact of eWOM on customers' decision-making processes can be more powerful than the impact of traditional WOM. In a study related to the B2B context, participants of the study recommended ask about recommending that the next successor continue using the supplier or the service provider (Stank et al., 2003). Thanks to the development of social media, B2B firms can capitalise on pre-existing business networks to spread WOM widely and to make their brands better known (Michaelidou, Siamagka and Christodoulides, 2011).

The relationship and impact on loyalty is mediated by a strong B2B brand through which companies are likely to achieve higher loyalty (McQuiston, 2004). From the study of Lacey and Morgan (2008), it emerges that loyal customers are more willing to contribute as customer advocates. B2B loyalty programme membership does not show any moderating effects on the model. For this reason, when loyalty programme membership is determined by the firm, business managers should not expect that this kind of programme improves customer advocacy behaviours. Advocacy towards the B2B partner is shown through sharing information, marketing research support, WOM referrals and

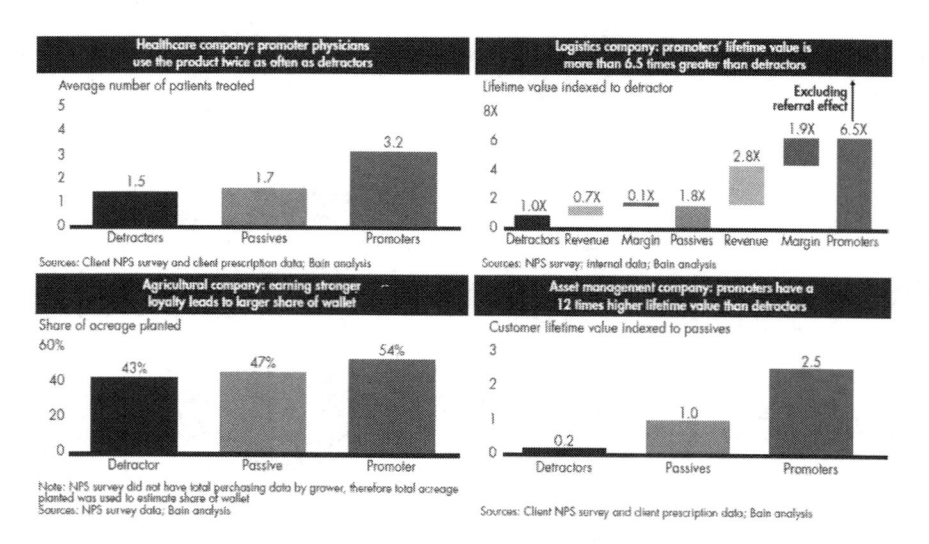

Figure 2.4 In B2B, promoters have a higher average lifetime value with respect to detractors

Source: Michels and Dullweber (2014)

patronage. It is the intention of the customer to help the partner grow. Loyal customers generally become voluntary marketing advocates.

Finally, a recent study by Bain into B2B companies reveals how customers who are 'promoters' have an average lifetime value ranging between 3 and 12 times that of 'detractors', depending on the segment and industry (see Figure 2.4). Thus, the effect of customer loyalty on WOM has been increasing over the last years; however, it needs further research particularly in the B2B context.

Note

1 http://cerasis.com/2014/02/20/history-of-reverse-logistics/

References

Anderson, E. W., Fornell, C. and Lehmann, D. R. (1994) 'Customer satisfaction, market share, and profitability: findings from Sweden', *Journal of Marketing*, 58(3), 53–66.

Anderson, E. W. and Weitz, B. (1992) 'The use of pledges to build and sustain commitment in distribution channels', *Journal of Marketing Research*, 29(1), 18–34.

Anderson, J. C. and Narus, J. A. (1984) 'A model of the distributor's perspective of distributor-manufacturer working relationships', *Journal of Marketing*, 48(4), 62–74.

Anderson, J. C., Narus, J. A. and Van Rossum, W. (2006) 'Customer value propositions in business markets', *Harvard Business Review*, 84(3), 90.

Arndt, J. (1967) 'Role of product-related conversations in the diffusion of a new product', *Journal of Marketing Research*, 4(3), 291–295.

Askariazad, M. H. and Babakhani, N. (2015) 'An application of European Customer Satisfaction Index (ECSI) in business to business (B2B) context', *Journal of Business & Industrial Marketing*, 30(1), 17–31.

Bell, S. J., Auh, S. and Smalley, K. (2005) 'Customer relationship dynamics: service quality and customer loyalty in the context of varying levels of customer expertise and switching costs', *Journal of the Academy of Marketing Science*, 33(2), 169–183.

Biong, H. (1993) 'Satisfaction and loyalty to suppliers within the grocery trade', *European Journal of Marketing*, 27(7), 21–38.

Black, T. (2014) *FedEx agrees to buy GENCO*. Available at www.bloomberg.com/news/articles/2014-12-15/fedex-agrees-to-buy-product-return-firm-genco-in-e-commerce-push. Accessed on 15th December 2016.

Blocker, C. P. and Flint, D. J. (2007) 'Customer segments as moving targets: integrating customer value dynamism into segment instability logic', *Industrial Marketing Management*, 36(6), 810–822.

Blocker, C. P., Flint, D. J., Myers, M. B. and Slater, S. F. (2011) 'Proactive customer orientation and its role for creating customer value in global markets', *Journal of the Academy of Marketing Science*, 39(2), 216–233.

Bloemer, J. and de Ruyter, K. (1999) 'Customer loyalty in high and low involvement service settings: the moderating impact of positive emotions', *Journal of Marketing Management*, 15(4), 315–330.

Blut, M., Beatty, S. E., Evanschitzky, H. and Brock, C. (2014) 'The impact of service characteristics on the switching costs – customer loyalty link', *Journal of Retailing*, 90(2), 275–290.

Blut, M., Evanschitzky, H., Backhaus, C., Rudd, J. and Marck, M. (2016) Securing business-to-business relationships: the impact of switching costs. *Industrial Marketing Management*, 52, 82–90.

Borghesi, A. and Gaudenzi, B. (2012) *Risk management: how to assess, transfer and communicate critical risks*, Milan: Springer Science & Business Media.

Bower, A. B. and Maxham III, J. G. (2012) 'Return shipping policies of online retailers: normative assumptions and the long-term consequences of fee and free returns', *Journal of Marketing*, 76(5), 110–124.

Brandenburg, M., Govindan, K., Sarkis, J. and Seuring, S. (2014) 'Quantitative models for sustainable supply chain management: developments and directions', *European Journal of Operational Research*, 233(2), 299–312.

Brock, J. L. (1934) 'The manufacturer's problem of returned merchandise', *Harvard Business Review*, 12(2), 253–260.

Bubb, P. L. and Van Rest, D. J. (1973) 'Loyalty as a component of the industrial buying decision', *Industrial Marketing Management*, 3(1), 25–32.

Burnham, T. A., Frels, J. K. and Mahajan, V. (2003) 'Consumer switching costs: a typology, antecedents, and consequences', *Journal of the Academy of Marketing Science*, 31(2), 109–126.

Cahill, D. L. (2006) Customer loyalty in third party logistics relationships: findings from studies in Germany and the USA. Physica, Heidelburg, Germany: Springer Science & Business Media.

Cahill, D. L., Goldsby, T. J., Knemeyer, A. M. and Wallenburg, C. M. (2010) 'Customer loyalty in logistics outsourcing relationships: an examination of the moderating effects of conflict frequency', *Journal of Business Logistics*, 31(2), 253–277.

Cambra-Fierro, J. J. and Polo-Redondo, Y. (2008) 'Creating satisfaction in the demand-supply chain: the buyers' perspective', *Supply Chain Management: An International Journal*, 13(3), 211–224.

Cater, B. and Cater, T. (2009) 'Relationship-value-based antecedents of customer satisfaction and loyalty in manufacturing', *Journal of Business & Industrial Marketing*, 24(8), 585–597.

Chiou, J.-S. and Droge, C. (2006) 'Service quality, trust, specific asset investment, and expertise: direct and indirect effects in a satisfaction-loyalty framework', *Journal of the Academy of Marketing Science*, 34(4), 613–627.

Christopher, M. (2016) *Logistics & supply chain management*, Harlow: Pearson Higher Education.

Christopher, M. and Peck, H. (2012) *Marketing logistics*, London: Routledge.

Chumpitaz Caceres, R. and Paparoidamis, N. G. (2007) 'Service quality, relationship satisfaction, trust, commitment and business-to-business loyalty', *European Journal of Marketing*, 41(7/8), 836–867.

Corsaro, D. and Snehota, I. (2010) 'Searching for relationship value in business markets: are we missing something?', *Industrial Marketing Management*, 39(6), 986–995.

Craighead, C. W., Karwan, K. R. and Miller, J. L. (2004) 'The effects of severity of failure and customer loyalty on service recovery strategies', *Production and Operations Management*, 13(4), 307–321.

Daugherty, P. J., Ellinger, A. E. and Plair, Q. J. (1997) 'Using service to create loyalty with key accounts', *International Journal of Logistics Management*, 8(2), 83–91.

Daugherty, P. J., Stank, T. P. and Ellinger, A. E. (1998) 'Leveraging logistics/distribution capabilities: the effect of logistics service on market share', *Journal of Business Logistics*, 19(2), 35.

Davis, B. R. and Mentzer, J. T. (2006) 'Logistics service driven loyalty: an exploratory study', *Journal of Business Logistics*, 27(2), 53–73.

Davis-Sramek, B., Mentzer, J. T. and Stank, T. P. (2008) 'Creating consumer durable retailer customer loyalty through order fulfillment service operations', *Journal of Operations Management*, 26(6), 781–797.

Day, G. S. (1969) 'A Two-Dimensional Concept of Brand Loyalty', *Journal of Advertising Research*, 9(3), 29–35.

De Ruyter, K., De Jong, A. and Wetzels, M. (2009) 'Antecedents and consequences of environmental stewardship in boundary-spanning B2B teams', *Journal of the Academy of Marketing Science*, 37(4), 470–487.

De Ruyter, K., Moorman, L. and Lemmink, J. (2001) 'Antecedents of commitment and trust in customer – supplier relationships in high technology markets', *Industrial Marketing Management*, 30(3), 271–286.

Dick, A. S. and Basu, K. (1994) 'Customer loyalty: toward an integrated conceptual framework', *Journal of the Academy of Marketing Science*, 22(2), 99–113.

Dwyer, F. R., Schurr, P. H. and Oh, S. (1987) 'Developing buyer-seller relationships', *Journal of Marketing*, 11–27.

Ellinger, A. E., Daugherty, P. J. and Plair, Q. J. (1999) 'Customer satisfaction and loyalty in supply chain: the role of communication', *Transportation Research Part E: Logistics and Transportation Review*, 35(2), 121–134.

Flint, D. J., Blocker, C. P. and Boutin, P. J. (2011) 'Customer value anticipation, customer satisfaction and loyalty: an empirical examination', *Industrial Marketing Management*, 40(2), 219–230.

Flint, D. J., Larsson, E., Gammelgaard, B. and Mentzer, J. T. (2005) 'Logistics innovation: a customer value-oriented social process', *Journal of Business Logistics*, 26(1), 113–147.

Flint, D. J. and Mentzer, J. T. (2000) 'Logiticians as marketers: their role when customers' desired value changes', *Journal of Business Logistics*, 21(2), 19.

Flint, D. J., Woodruff, R. B. and Gardial, S. F. (1997) 'Customer value change in industrial marketing relationships: a call for new strategies and research', *Industrial Marketing Management*, 26(2), 163–175.

Fornell, C. (1992) 'A national customer satisfaction barometer: the Swedish experience', *Journal of Marketing*, 56(1), 6–21.

Frazier, G. L. (May 1983) 'On the measurement of interfirm power in channels of distribution', *Journal of Marketing Research*, 20(2), 158–166.

Ganesh, J., Arnold, M. J. and Reynolds, K. E. (2000) 'Understanding the customer base of service providers: an examination of the differences between switchers and stayers', *Journal of Marketing*, 64(3), 65–87.

Gassenheimer, J. B., Sterling, J. U. and Robicheaux, R. A. (1989) 'Long-term channel member relationships', *International Journal of Physical Distribution & Materials Management*, 19(12), 15–28.

Geiger, I., Durand, A., Saab, S., Kleinaltenkamp, M., Baxter, R. and Lee, Y. (2012) 'The bonding effects of relationship value and switching costs in industrial buyer – seller relationships: an investigation into role differences', *Industrial Marketing Management*, 41(1), 82–93.

Govindan, K., Soleimani, H. and Kannan, D. (2015) 'Reverse logistics and closed-loop supply chain: a comprehensive review to explore the future', *European Journal of Operational Research*, 240(3), 603–626. doi:10.1016/j.ejor.2014.07.012.

Greve, C. and Davis, J. (2012) An executive's guide to reverse logistics: how to find hidden profits by managing returns, Pittsburgh, PA: Greve Davis Publishing, Inc.

Grönroos, C. and Ravald, A. (2011) 'Service as business logic: implications for value creation and marketing', *Journal of Service Management*, 22(1), 5–22.

Grönroos, C. and Voima, P. (2013) 'Critical service logic: making sense of value creation and co-creation', *Journal of the Academy of Marketing Science*, 41(2), 133–150.

Guenzi, P. and Pelloni, O. (2004) 'The impact of interpersonal relationships on customer satisfaction and loyalty to the service provider', *International Journal of Service Industry Management*, 15(4), 365–384.

Gundlach, G. T., Achrol, R. S. and Mentzer, J. T. (1995) 'The structure of commitment in exchange', *Journal of Marketing*, 59(1), 78–92.

Gupta, S., Hanssens, D., Hardie, B., Kahn, W., Kumar, V., Lin, N., Ravishanker, N. and Sriram, S. (2006) 'Modeling customer lifetime value', *Journal of Service Research*, 9(2), 139–155.

Hart, C. W. and Johnson, M. D. (1999) 'Growing the trust relationship', *Marketing Management*, 8(1), 8–18.

Hartmann, E. and De Grahl, A. (2011) 'The flexibility of logistics service providers and its impact on customer loyalty: an empirical study', *Journal of Supply Chain Management*, 47(3), 63–85.

Hazen, B. T., Hall, D. J. and Hanna, J. B. (2012) 'Reverse logistics disposition decision-making: developing a decision framework via content analysis', *International Journal of Physical Distribution & Logistics Management*, 42(3), 244–274.

Hazen, B. T., Overstreet, R. E., Hall, D. J., Huscroft, J. R. and Hanna, J. B. (2015) 'Antecedents to and outcomes of reverse logistics metrics', *Industrial Marketing Management*, 46, 160–170.

Heide, J. B. and Weiss, A. M. (1995) 'Vendor consideration and switching behavior for buyers in high-technology markets', *Journal of Marketing*, 59(3), 30–43.

Heinonen, K., Helkkula, A., Holmlund-Rytkönen, M., Selos, E., Laine, T., Roos, I., Suomala, P. and Pitkänen, L. (2013) 'Applying SPAT for understanding B-to-B supplier switching processes', *Managing Service Quality: An International Journal*, 23(4), 321–340.

Hennig-Thurau, T., Malthouse, E. C., Friege, C., Gensler, S., Lobschat, L., Rangaswamy, A. and Skiera, B. (2010) 'The impact of new media on customer relationships', *Journal of Service Research*, 13(3), 311–330.

Hewett, K., Money, R. B. and Sharma, S. (2002) 'An exploration of the moderating role of buyer corporate culture in industrial buyer-seller relationships', *Journal of the Academy of Marketing Science*, 30(3), 229–239.

Holbrook, M. B. (1994) 'The nature of customer value: An axiology of services in the consumption experience. In R.T. Rust and R.L. Oliver (Eds.), *Service Quality: New Directions in Theory and Practice*. Thousand Oaks, CA: Sage.

Homburg, C. and Fürst, A. (2005) 'How organizational complaint handling drives customer loyalty: an analysis of the mechanistic and the organic approach', *Journal of Marketing*, 69(3), 95–114.

Homburg, C. and Giering, A. (2001) 'Personal characteristics as moderators of the relationship between customer satisfaction and loyalty – an empirical analysis', *Psychology & Marketing*, 18(1), 43–66.

Homburg, C., Koschate, N. and Hoyer, W. D. (2005) 'Do satisfied customers really pay more? a study of the relationship between customer satisfaction and willingness to pay', *Journal of Marketing*, 69(2), 84–96.

Homburg, C. and Stock, R. M. (2005) 'Exploring the conditions under which salesperson work satisfaction can lead to customer satisfaction', *Psychology & Marketing*, 22(5), 393–420.

Huang, Y. C., Yang, M. L. and Wong, Y. J. (2016) 'Institutional pressures, resources commitment, and returns management', *Supply Chain Management: An International Journal*, 21(3), 398–416.

Innis, D. E. and La Londe, B. J. (1994) 'Customer service: the key to customer satisfaction, customer loyalty, and market share', *Journal of Business Logistics*, 15(1), 1–28.

Janita, M. S. and Miranda, F. J. (2013) 'The antecedents of client loyalty in business-to-business (B2B) electronic marketplaces', *Industrial Marketing Management*, 42(5), 814–823.

Jap, S. D. and Ganesan, S. (2000) 'Control mechanisms and the relationship life cycle: implications for safeguarding specific investments and developing commitment', *Journal of Marketing Research*, 37(2), 227–245.

Klemperer, P. (1995) 'Competition when consumers have switching costs: an overview with applications to industrial organization, macroeconomics, and international trade', *Review of Economic Studies*, 62(4), 515–539.

Kumar, V. (2008) *Customer lifetime value: the path to profitability*, Delfft, The Netherlands: NOW Publishers Inc.

Kwon, I. G. and Suh, T. (2004) 'Factors affecting the level of trust and commitment in supply chain relationships', *Journal of Supply Chain Management*, 40(1), 4–14.

Lacey, R. and Morgan, R. M. (2008) 'Customer advocacy and the impact of B2B loyalty programs', *Journal of Business & Industrial Marketing*, 24(1), 3–13.

Lam, S. Y., Shankar, V., Erramilli, M. K. and Murthy, B. (2004) 'Customer value, satisfaction, loyalty, and switching costs: an illustration from a business-to-business service context', *Journal of the Academy of Marketing Science*, 32(3), 293–311.

Lambert, D. M. and Harrington, T. C. (1989) 'Establishing customer service strategies within the marketing mix: More empirical evidence', *Journal of Business Logistics*, 10(2), 44–72.

Langley, C. J. and Capgemini (2015) *Third-party logistics study: the state of logistics outsourcing*. Results and Findings of the 19th Annual Study. Available at www.3plstudy.com. Accessed on 17th December 2015.

Lapierre, J. (2000) 'Customer-perceived value in industrial contexts', *Journal of Business and Industrial Marketing*, 15(2–3), 122–140.

Large, R. O., Kramer, N. and Hartmann, R. K. (2011) 'Customer-specific adaptation by providers and their perception of 3PL-relationship success', *International Journal of Physical Distribution & Logistics Management*, 41(9), 822–838.

Lepak, D. P., Smith, K. G. and Taylor, M. S. (2007) 'Value creation and value capture: a multilevel perspective', *Academy of Management Review*, 32(1), 180–194.

Leuschner, R., Carter, C. R., Goldsby, T. J. and Rogers, Z. S. (2014) 'Third-party logistics: a meta-analytic review and investigation of its impact on performance', *Journal of Supply Chain Management*, 50(1), 21–43.

Lewis, R. C. and Booms, B. H. (1983) 'The marketing aspects of service quality', in Leonard L. Berry, G. Lynn Shostack and Gregory Upah (eds), *Emerging perspectives on services marketing*, Chicago: American Marketing Association, 99–107.

Li, Y., Wei, C. and Cai, X. (2012) 'Optimal pricing and order policies with B2B product returns for fashion products', *International Journal of Production Economics*, 135(2), 637–646.

Lin, F., Lo, Y. and Sung, Y. (2006) 'Effects of switching cost, trust, and information sharing on supply chain performance for B2B e-commerce: A multi-agent simulation study, 2006. Proceedings of the 39th Annual Hawaii International Conference on System Sciences (HICSS'06), IEEE, 105b–105b, 4–7. Washington, DC: January. IEEE Conference Publications..

Lindgreen, A., Hingley, M. K., Grant, D. B. and Morgan, R. E. (2012) 'Value in business and industrial marketing: past, present, and future', *Industrial Marketing Management*, 41(1), 207–214.

Maignan, I., Ferrell, O. C. and Hult, G. T. M. (1999) 'Corporate citizenship: cultural antecedents and business benefits', *Journal of the Academy of Marketing Science*, 27(4), 455–469.

Matzler, K., Strobl, A., Thurner, N. and Füller, J. (2015) 'Switching experience, customer satisfaction, and switching costs in the ICT industry', *Journal of Service Management*, 26(1), 117–136.

McQuiston, D. H. (2004) 'Successful branding of a commodity product: The case of RAEX LASER steel', *Industrial Marketing Management*, 33(4), 345–354.

Mentzer, J. T., Flint, D. J. and Hult, G. T. M. (2001) 'Logistics service quality as a segment-customized process', *Journal of Marketing*, 65(4), 82–104. doi:10.1509/jmkg.65.4.82.18390.

Merrilees, B. and Fenech, T. (2007) 'From catalog to Web: B2B multi-channel marketing strategy', *Industrial Marketing Management*, 36(1), 44–49.

Michaelidou, N., Siamagka, N. T. and Christodoulides, G. (2011) 'Usage, barriers and measurement of social media marketing: an exploratory investigation of small and medium B2B brands', *Industrial Marketing Management*, 40(7), 1153–1159.

Michels, D. and Dullweber, A. (2014) *Do your B2B customers promote your business?* Available at www.bain.com/publications/articles/do-your-b2b-customers-promote-your-business.aspx. Accessed on 12th January 2017.

Mittal, B. and Lassar, W. M. (1998) 'Why do customers switch? The dynamics of satisfaction versus loyalty', *Journal of Services Marketing*, 12(3), 177–194.

Molinari, L. K., Abratt, R. and Dion, P. (2008) 'Satisfaction, quality and value and effects on repurchase and positive word-of-mouth behavioral intentions in a B2B services context', *Journal of Services Marketing*, 22(5), 363–373.

Mollenkopf, D. A., Frankel, R. and Russo, I. (2011) 'Creating value through returns management: exploring the marketing-operations interface', *Journal of Operations Management*, 29(5), 391–403.

Mollenkopf, D. A., Frankel, R. and Russo, I. (2016) 'Sell right, not more: leveraging internet integration to mitigate product returns', in Chad W. Autry and Mark A. Moon (eds), *Achieving supply chain integration: connecting the supply chain inside and out for competitive advantage*, Old Tappan, NJ: Pearson FT Press.

Mollenkopf, D. A., Rabinovich, E., Laseter, T. M. and Boyer, K. K. (2007) 'Managing internet product returns: a focus on effective service operations', *Decision Sciences*, 38(2), 215–250.

Morgan, R. M. and Hunt, S. D. (1994) 'The commitment-trust theory of relationship marketing', *Journal of Marketing*, 58(3), 20–38.

National Retail Federation. (2015) *Consumer returns in the retail industry*. Available at https://nrf.com/sites/default/files/Images/Media%20Center/NRF%20Retail%20Return%20Fraud%20Final_0.pdf. Accessed on 20th December 2016.

Naumann, E., Williams, P. and Khan, M. S. (2009) 'Customer satisfaction and loyalty in B2B services: directions for future research', *Marketing Review*, 9(4), 319–333.

Nielson, C. C. (1996) 'An empirical examination of switching cost investments in business-to-business marketing relationships', *Journal of Business & Industrial Marketing*, 11(6), 38–60.

Oliva, T. A., Oliver, R. L. and MacMillan, I. C. (1992) 'A catastrophe model for developing service satisfaction strategies', *Journal of Marketing*, 56(3), 83–95.

Oliver, R. L. (1999) 'Whence consumer loyalty?', *Journal of Marketing*, 63, 33–44.

Oliver, R. L., Rust, R. T. and Varki, S. (1997) 'Customer delight: foundations, findings, and managerial insight', *Journal of Retailing*, 73(3), 311–336.

Palmatier, R. W., Scheer, L. K. and Steenkamp, J.-B. E. M. (2007) 'Customer loyalty to whom? Managing the benefits and risks of salesperson-owned loyalty', *Journal of Marketing Research*, 44(2), 185–199. doi:10.1509/jmkr.44.2.185.

Parasuraman, A., Berry, L. L. and Zeithaml, V. A. (1991) 'Refinement and reassessment of the SERVQUAL scale', *Journal of Retailing*, 67(4), 420.

Park, J.-G., Park, K. and Lee, J. (2014) 'A firm's post-adoption behavior: loyalty or switching costs?', *Industrial Management & Data Systems*, 114(2), 258–275.

Petersen, J. A., Anderson, E. T., Kumar, V. and Shah, D. (2015) 'Leveraging product returns to maximize customer equity', in V. Kumar and Denish Shah (eds), *Handbook of research on customer equity in marketing*, Cheltenham: Edward Elgar Publishing, 160–177.

Petersen, J. A. and Kumar, V. (2009) 'Are product returns a necessary evil? antecedents and consequences', *Journal of Marketing*, 73(3), 35–51.

Pick, D. and Eisend, M. (2014) 'Buyers' perceived switching costs and switching: a meta-analytic assessment of their antecedents', *Journal of the Academy of Marketing Science*, 42(2), 186–204.

Pollock, W. K. (2007) 'Using reverse logistics to enhance customer service and competitive performance', *Reverse Logistics Magazine*. Available at www.reverselogisticstrends.com/rlmagazine/edition08p12.php. Accessed on 10th December 2016.

Rafiq, M. and Jaafar, H. S. (2007) 'Measuring customers' perceptions of logistics service quality of 3PL service providers', *Journal of Business Logistics*, 28(2), 159–175.

Ramaseshan, B., Rabbanee, F. K. and Tan Hsin Hui, L. (2013) 'Effects of customer equity drivers on customer loyalty in B2B context', *Journal of Business & Industrial Marketing*, 28(4), 335–346.

Rauyruen, P. and Miller, K. E. (2007) 'Relationship quality as a predictor of B2B customer loyalty', *Journal of Business Research*, 60(1), 21–31.

Ritter, T. and Andersen, H. (2014) 'A relationship strategy perspective on relationship portfolios: linking customer profitability, commitment, and growth potential to relationship strategy', *Industrial Marketing Management*, 43(6), 1005–1011.

Ritter, T. and Walter, A. (2012) 'More is not always better: the impact of relationship functions on customer-perceived relationship value', *Industrial Marketing Management*, 41(1), 136–144.

Roenisch, S. (15 February 2013), *Onlinehandel: Wege aus dem Retourendilemma*. Available at www.ibusiness.de/members/aktuell/db/581766SUR.html. Accessed on February 2014.

Rogers, D. S., Melamed, B. and Lembke, R. S. (2012) 'Modeling and analysis of reverse logistics', *Journal of Business Logistics*, 33(2), 107–117. doi:10.1111/j.0000-0000.2012.01043.x.

Rubio, S., Chamorro, A. and Miranda, F. J. (2008) 'Characteristics of the research on reverse logistics (1995–2005)', *International Journal of Production Research*, 46(4), 1099–1120. Taylor & Francis.

Russo, I., Confente, I., Gligor, D. M. and Autry, C. W. (2016) 'To be or not to be (loyal): is there a recipe for customer loyalty in the B2B context?', *Journal of Business Research*, 69(2), 888–896. doi:10.1016/j.jbusres.2015.07.002.

Russo, I., Confente, I., Gligor, D. M., & Cobelli, N. (2017). 'The combined effect of product returns experience and switching costs on B2B customer re-purchase intent', *Journal of Business & Industrial Marketing*, 32(5).

Rust, R. T. and Zahorik, A. J. (1993) 'Customer satisfaction, customer retention, and market share', *Journal of Retailing*, 69(2), 193–215.

Sánchez, J. Á. L., Vijande, M. L. S. and Gutiérrez, J. A. T. (2011) 'The effects of manufacturer's organizational learning on distributor satisfaction and loyalty in industrial markets', *Industrial Marketing Management*, 40(4), 624–635.

Scheer, L. K., Miao, C. F. and Garrett, J. (2010) 'The effects of supplier capabilities on industrial customers' loyalty: the role of dependence', *Journal of the Academy of Marketing Science*, 38(1), 90–104.

Selnes, F. and Gønhaug, K. (2000) 'Effects of supplier reliability and benevolence in business marketing', *Journal of Business Research*, 49(3), 259–271.

Shong-lee Ivan Su, D., Huo, B., Liu, C., Kang, M. and Zhao, X. (2015) 'The impact of dependence and relationship commitment on logistics outsourcing: empirical evidence from Greater China', *International Journal of Physical Distribution & Logistics Management*, 45(9/10), 887–912.

Slater, S. F. (1997) 'Developing a customer value-based theory of the firm', *Journal of the Academy of Marketing Science*, 25(2), 162–167.

Smith, J. B. and Colgate, M. (2007) 'Customer value creation: a practical framework', *Journal of Marketing Theory and Practice*, 15(1), 7–23.

Stank, T. P., Goldsby, T. J. and Vickery, S. K. (1999) 'Effect of service supplier performance on satisfaction and loyalty of store managers in the fast food industry', *Journal of Operations Management*, 17(4), 429–447.

Stank, T. P., Goldsby, T. J., Vickery, S. K. and Savitskie, K. (2003) 'Logistics service performance: estimating its influence on market share', *Journal of Business Logistics*, 24(1), 27–55.

Stank, T. P., Pellathy, D.A., In, J., Mollenkopf, D.A. and Bell, J.E. (2017). 'New frontiers in logistics research: Theorizing at the middle range', *Journal of Business Logistics*, 38(1), 6–17.

Stock, J. R. and Lambert, D. M. (2001) *Strategic logistics management*, Boston, MA: McGraw-Hill/Irwin.

Thai, V. V. (2013) 'Logistics service quality: conceptual model and empirical evidence', *International Journal of Logistics Research and Applications*, 16(2), 114–131.

Tsai, M.-T., Tsai, C.-L. and Chang, H.-C. (2010) 'The effect of customer value, customer satisfaction, and switching costs on customer loyalty: an empirical study of hypermarkets in Taiwan', *Social Behavior and Personality: An International Journal*, 38(6), 729–740.

Ulaga, W. (2003) 'Capturing value creation in business relationships: a customer perspective', *Industrial Marketing Management*, 32(8), 677–693.

Ulaga, W. and Eggert, A. (2006a) 'Relationship value and relationship quality', *European Journal of Marketing*, 40(3/4), 311–327.

Ulaga, W. and Eggert, A. (2006b) 'Value-based differentiation in business relationships: gaining and sustaining key supplier status', *Journal of Marketing*, 70(1), 119–136. doi:10.1509/jmkg.2006.70.1.119.

Van Thienen, S., Delesalle, P., Overdulve, K. and Vandevelde, S. (2014) *The hidden value in reverse logistics point of view*, Deloitte Consulting, Creative Studio at Deloitte, Belgium. Available at https://www2.deloitte.com/content/dam/Deloitte/be/Documents/process-and-operations/BE_POV_Supply-chain-strategy_20140109.pdf. Accessed on 12th November 2016.

Verbeke, W., Dietz, B. and Verwaal, E. (2011) 'Drivers of sales performance: a contemporary meta-analysis: have salespeople become knowledge brokers?', *Journal of the Academy of Marketing Science*, 39(3), 407–428.

Verhoef, P. C. (2003) 'Understanding the effect of customer relationship management efforts on customer retention and customer share development', *Journal of Marketing*, 67(4), 30–45.

Wagner, S. M. and Friedl, G. (2007) 'Supplier switching decisions', *European Journal of Operational Research*, 183(2), 700–717.

Wallenburg, C. M., Cahill, D. L., Michael Knemeyer, A. and Goldsby, T. J. (2011) 'Commitment and trust as drivers of loyalty in logistics outsourcing relationships: cultural differences between the United States and Germany', *Journal of Business Logistics*, 32(1), 83–98.

Walsh, G., Albrecht, A. K., Kunz, W. and Hofacker, C. F. (2016) 'Relationship between online retailers' reputation and product returns', *British Journal of Management*, 27(1), 3–20.

Wangenheim, F. and Bayón, T. (2004) 'The effect of word of mouth on services switching: measurement and moderating variables', *European Journal of Marketing*, 38(9/10), 1173–1185.

Watson, G. F., Beck, J. T., Henderson, C. M. and Palmatier, R. W. (2015) 'Building, measuring, and profiting from customer loyalty', *Journal of the Academy of Marketing Science*, 43(6), 790–825. doi:10.1007/s11747-015-0439-4.

Wetzels, M., De Ruyter, K. and Van Birgelen, M. (1998) 'Marketing service relationships: the role of commitment', *Journal of Business & Industrial Marketing*, 13(4/5), 406–423.

Whitten, D. and Wakefield, R. L. (2006) 'Measuring switching costs in IT outsourcing services', *Journal of Strategic Information Systems*, 15(3), 219–248.

Wind, Y. (November 1970) 'Industrial source loyalty', *Journal of Marketing Research*, 7(4), 450–457.

Woisetschläger, D. M., Lentz, P. and Evanschitzky, H. (2011) 'How habits, social ties, and economic switching barriers affect customer loyalty in contractual service settings', *Journal of Business Research*, 64(8), 800–808.

3 The era of omnichannel

From offline to online: the impact of digitalisation

> Whereas before they came here with these bags and flushed out every pair of shoes . . . now even the customers got used over time, and we allowed them: ok, send me an email, let me see what the problem is, we solve it, if we can't send me over the defect product, we need to manage and to keep the relationships . . . There is a much more direct and continuous contact with the customers in the era of digitalisation, in the era of iPad . . . it is very accelerated the demand of any kind . . . replenishment order, delivery times until product returns.

This is a very recent comment by a global fashion company's director of operations. From his voice can be deduced one of the many impacts digitalisation has on operations and SCM. Thus, the rapid growth of information and communication technology (ICT) has radically altered the way people collect information, evaluate consumption alternatives, the way they shop every day. To mention just a few numbers: people accessing the Web via multiple devices, from mobile phones to computers and other devices, has reached over 3 billion in 2016, counting almost 40% of the population worldwide (Internetlivestats, 2016).

This implies that people also shop using several devices and do not merely go to the closest store. Such behaviour leads the online retail context to be in continuous evolution, with estimations that online sales will account for more than 12% by 2019 – more than doubled compared with online sales registered in 2015 (Nielsen, 2016). Digitalisation has rapidly changed not only how we buy but also how and where we review products and services, and the way we communicate with other people and with the brands. From sensors and cloud services to nanotech, big data and real-time data, several technologies drive digital trends also in the B2B industry. How fast this digital technology enables advances in performance and costs will determine how quickly they bring changes in managing supply chains (Sanders, 2014).

In this sense, digital technology has already dramatically changed firms' operations, logistical activities, communication and marketing strategies and their relationships with suppliers and customers, as well as the way in which customers are served. Such changes have also influenced consumers to be more collaborative and interactive. Thus, consumers are not just passive individuals to whom a company must propose a product or a service, but are an integrated partner of the company (Lusch and Vargo, 2014). With the emergence of new technologies and e-business models, the role of the customer is being transformed from a passive buyer to an active participant in co-creating value. This 'proactivity' has led to a proliferation of online feedback, more accessible and visible data about orders and product returns, information about brands, products and services preferences, and choices. Such data can be very useful for companies and for SCM. Indeed, supply chain managers are increasingly reliant upon data to gain visibility into expenditures, identify trends in costs and performance and support process control, inventory monitoring, and production optimisation and process improvement efforts. In fact, many businesses are awash with data, with many seeking to capitalise on data analysis as a means for gaining a competitive advantage (Hazen, Boone, Ezell and Jones-Farmer, 2014).

Samplings of user feedback show that transactions between partners connected on the social network result in significantly higher user satisfaction, bringing the supply chain into a new era. The potential of tools such as the feedback system and the Facebook 'like' button is huge and it can easily be moved from e-commerce platforms to B2B e-market and e-procurement platforms. The primary objective of Supply 2.0 is to support internal and external information and communication processes and to ensure that relevant information is available in companies and supply chains through the use of lightweight technology (Christopher and Holweg, 2011).

The importance of integration and synchronisation of data and communications to and by the customer represents a hot topic for several companies we have met over the years, as this operations manager of a global manufacturer for the propulsion system marine application industry sector highlighted:

> I understood the customer was changing because the end user was requesting a system completely different from the time . . . we have to change our process. After this, one year as we set in all the processes we arrived at a very good situation and the customer was very satisfied . . . What was a mistake in the past was that our customers were between us and the end user. They were talking to the end user and that was supposed to be enough for them to understand. We were close to the end user and I started to push, push, after that problem with the product, this is a problem that we could avoid. So, the one problem with communication is now this. Avoid any circle and go in a straight line to the customer.

The digital transformation should help companies to be more integrated and in contact with the customers, and with the customers of the customers, until the end users. Such changes have several implications for companies and the B2B context must deal with this transformation to digital as well. In response to these changes, research has focused on designing new supply chain models and multichannel and governance strategies to improve results. Faster replenishment times, quicker times to market and shorter delivery times have been shown to improve the performance of entire value chains and enhance customer satisfaction and loyalty.

Another issue is related to the consequences of online shopping growth for shopping in a physical store. The digital revolution has transformed forecast consumer purchasing paths into several touchpoints to be covered; thus, the B2B method of selling has also become less predictive as customers research, evaluate, select, repeat and share experiences about products. Both theory and practice could be enriched if research aimed to develop a better understanding of how digital technologies can most effectively be used to manage supply chains (Waller and Fawcett, 2013; Richey Jr, Morgan, Lindsey-Hall and Adams, 2016). Traditional manufacturers and retailers need to create supply chains, operation models and multichannel strategies to meet online and offline requirements.

As Andrew Shaw, Ducab's Managing Director leading manufacturers of energy cables in the Middle East, describes:

> There's a temptation to see digitisation as being most significant in consumer-facing markets, but it's equally relevant for manufacturers like us in a B2B environment. The momentum of change is gathering pace, through initiatives with suppliers and customers and the opportunity for cost savings.
>
> (Khurana and Al-Olama, 2016)

Today, distribution channel systems are increasingly complex, as producers must serve their end-user markets through multiple channels and partners. Under such systems, the level of complexity increases, as firms must choose between different business models that rely on different technological choices. The so-called Industry 4.0[1] will change the whole supply chain; through the integration with suppliers and logistics optimisation, transaction costs and inventory levels can be lower. A better use of smart labels and a more comprehensive use of data will track and trace inventory on site and in transit to customers; in brief, there is the chance to gain some competitive advantage for first movers.

Moreover, with the advent of e-commerce and e-procurement, the need for specific skills and competencies in the outsourcing context has created new challenges in the inter-organisational context of customer-supplier relationships. Thus, a firm may outsource its services to enhance its customer services and flexibility by negotiating with a third party with specific expertise for the provision of non-core services. Subsequently, a large part of governing supply chains comprises managing and governing multiple relationships among member organisations.

Within this context, technology can act as one of the primary facilitators of a supply chain excellence strategy. Yet great care must be exercised in selecting and applying technology within a context as complex as the extended supply chain in the new era. One of the ways to improve the benefits of the supply chain competition is through the use of advanced ICT tools available on the market, harnessing them into a decision dashboard. For example, supply chain integration is the most important factor that derives effects from e-procurement to SCM, implying that supply chain integration represents the main reason to explain the processes through which e-procurement contributes to supply chain performance (Hsin Chang, Tsai and Hsu, 2013). Consequently, a number of important questions in the operationalisation of omnichannel strategies have needed to be delivered, basically because the traditional supply chain is not a good fit for the purpose of omnichannel.

For example: is one channel replacing the other? If not, how can brick-and-mortar and online contexts work together to enhance companies' performance and at the same time satisfy the customer? The answer is that consumers do not merely visit the store and then go digital to look for the lowest-cost offer, they search for information and evaluate alternatives online while deciding to purchase the product in-store. Such integration of channels requires a rethink of company strategies, not only from a marketing perspective, understanding the customer's journey and suggesting the right offer in the right place, but also from a logistics perspective, from order to delivery to the final customer (Kwon and Lennon, 2009).

The three top activities that consumers like to do online are: search information about products and services, compare among alternatives (in particular, prices) and search for discounts or coupon and special deals. For instance, considering the products or services, consumers are more likely to search for information online. A recent study found that consumer electronics and travel products online are the most searched products prior to purchase, while for consumable goods such as groceries or beauty products the percentage is lower than for durable goods (Nielsen, 2016).

In the same study, that might be interesting to explore, is what consumers do *not* do online. Surprisingly, the lowest rate (about 10% of the respondents) was given to the usage of the following activities or tools: the usage of online advertisements, to clicking a store email and liking, tweeting or commenting about a product or a brand. Such results are opposed to what companies rely on for the Web, and further investigation is required to understand better what consumers like and get engaged with and what they dislike in relation to online channels.

What the online context has reinforced is that customers are loyal to experiences, not to companies. This does not mean it has killed loyalty, but it has shown new models of loyalty based on experience rather than brands, products and companies. Recently, sales models took the form of a classic sales and marketing funnel in which customers moved in a linear fashion from discovery to consideration to evaluation to purchase. The key point was the 'purchase' action for companies, which secured loyalty. Consequently, all the company's investment efforts into building loyalty were concentrated in this phase, through discounts, rebates and offers. The common belief was that once the customer was acquired she or he would stick with the company. Digitalisation has brought more dynamism to customers, providing them with more information, opinions and opportunities, and lower costs to access to new companies, products and

offers. Digitalisation has also shed more light on what leads to customer retention, based more on experience than transaction. This is the quality of experience customers perceive before, during and after sales and is confirmed by a
recent study, which found:

- 65% of consumers use online channels – not primarily for price advantages,
  but for convenience, speed, the quality of information provided and access
  to a broader range of choices.
- 60% find 'being promised one thing and delivered something else' the most
  frustrating experience they can have with a company.
- 65% (nearly 80% in emerging markets) have switched at least one provider
  in the past year because of poor service.
- 82% of 'switchers' believe companies could have retained them with better
  experiences and more accurate expectations.

(Quiring and Schunck, 2015)

Although the reasons that lead consumers to purchase online vary from person to person and are based on the product or service and other variables, in
Table 3.1 we attempt to summarise the main benefits (Forsythe, Liu, Shannon
and Gardner, 2006; Escobar-Rodríguez and Carvajal-Trujillo, 2013; Jiang, Yan
and Jun, 2013) that motivate and the main challenges that limit consumers to
purchase online.

Consequently, consumers' choices and perceptions have a huge impact on the
supply chain, where decisions must be taken regardless the channels, products
and services; operations need to be reorganised to succeed in the two channels, considering the perceived benefits and barriers from purchasing from the
channels. Table 3.1 summarises the main barriers consumers face when buying
online. Such barriers have a heavy impact on B2B operations and supply strategies as they might lead suppliers to revise their returns policies to lower the risk
of not trying the product, to extend the guarantee of products and to revise
their delivery options.

From multichannel to omnichannel – the company perspective

Digitalisation has not only changed purchasing habits but has also affected the
entire supply chain system. The supply chain today is a series of several nodes,
siloed steps taken through upstream raw material via sourcing, plan, design and
production, logistics distribution, sales and finally into the hands of the customer. Digitisation potentially brings down those walls, and the supply chain
becomes a completely integrated ecosystem that is fully transparent to all the
members involved.

Consumers integrate digital touchpoints within the traditional offline journey to purchase, from reading online reviews about products to using their
mobile phone apps to purchase or to ask advice from online shopping assistants.

Table 3.1 Drivers and barriers to buying online

Drivers	Barriers
Convenience: Not intended as money saving but rather time and effort reduction to collect information about products and brand, and a faster buying decision process.	*Quality concern and product inspection:* The inability to inspect products represents one of the main barriers for consumers. However, this barrier can be lower if consumers feel free to easily return the product. The challenge is the guarantee from suppliers/intermediaries' ad hoc lenient returns policies for the online context.
Informed decision-making: Making better buying decisions by being better informed through online content provided by companies and peer reviews (electronic WOM).	*No money saving:* Many consumers believe that a price incentive is the only reason to shop online, particularly for consumer electronics and mobile products. However, sometimes it is not easy to have a comparison among offline and online prices. To fill this gap, in the United States, some big companies are already matching online prices, and many stores offer in-store advice and the opportunity to touch and try the products. This can decrease the barrier to purchase online. In addition, to facilitate online shopping, some retailers are including free shipping for first-time users, double points for loyalty programme members or online/mobile exclusive offers.
Product assortment: Consumers can have access to a wider assortment of products particularly offered by companies that they cannot reach locally. This, of course, implies a great opportunity for suppliers to boost sales.	*Restrictive returns policy:* A lenient return policy plays an important role in persuading consumers to buy a product online. In addition, it lowers the risk linked to quality concerns. This allows consumers to receive a meaningful guarantee that in the case of an unsatisfying experience with the product because of different problems (not the right size, wrong product delivered, incomplete order, etc.), she or he can return the product in an easy and cheap way.
Deal seeking: Being easier and faster to compare alternatives and brands, consumers can also find the best deal in terms of price/discounts and coupons.	*Delivery problems:* Another issue related to online purchasing is the concern about delivery, e.g., if the product arrives when consumers are not at home. This barrier can be overcome with a proper reengineering fulfilment process that allows better forecasting for online shoppers' needs, extending delivery windows or providing other ways to deliver and pick up the product beyond home (delivery lockers, in-store delivery, etc.).
Useful online features: Managing shopping lists and filling baskets over time.	*Lack of social engagement:* This barrier can be perceived in particular for certain product categories, where store experience might play a key role in a consumer's buying decision. This is the case for books or music for instance, where consumers can perceive a pleasure from interacting with salespeople in the store and with other consumers.
	Lack of trust: This remains a problem as consumers can feel unsafe when providing their personal information online. Concern about security and privacy presents a critical point, particularly for older consumers.
	Poor telecommunications infrastructures and technology adoption: Although many of the countries around the world have high rates of Internet penetration, technology adoption and online shopping can vary based on costs to access the Internet and on the speediness of connections.

This behaviour implies consumers switch between offline and online channels in an easy way. Such experiences have significant consequences from a managerial point of view because companies, and particularly retailers, must offer such experiences in a seamless and fluid way. This convergence of different channels is challenging companies that on one hand need to satisfy consumers, and on the other they need to aim at being profitable and efficient (Cummins, Peltier and Dixon, 2016).

Multichannel marketing relates to the practice of communicating with and offering buyers goods and services via two or more synchronised channels (Rangaswamy and Van Bruggen, 2005). The aim of multichannel marketers is to effectively manage customer relationships according to customers' channel preference, catalogues, direct mail, phone or digital channels, including e-commerce and mobile devices (Kushwaha and Shankar, 2013). Channels include brick and mortar retail operations. The term 'omnichannel' means to combine in an integrated way different channels, both online and offline, from mobile to brick and mortar and a mix of devices. Customers move freely between in-store, traditional out-of-store and online communications as part of a single transaction environment.

The omnichannel approach requires companies to redefine their supply strategy and business models. As working separately for each channel can no longer be sustainable, companies that have been traditional brick and mortar are looking to go online while, at the same time, e-tailers are trying various options to establish a physical presence, for example showrooms and pop-up stores, either temporary or permanent. The challenge is to find a seamless solution for both the customer experience and internal processes (Ternstrand, Selldin, Virta, and Linder, 2015). The omnichannel strategy ends the era of online channels that are thought of and treated as a separate channel without integration to the traditional channel. If done properly, a omnichannel experience blurs the distinctions between physical and online interactivity, providing customer with 'no wall' stores (Cummins et al., 2016).

This happens because, no matter the channel, companies need to respond to the changing marketplace and to meet growing customer demands. In fact, customers want to access at any time and at any place the information about their orders, the delivery status or the level of the stock. Even though they may be in a physical store, they have access to mobile or other devices and they search for information, thus integrating their buying experience. Previous studies confirmed that multichannel shoppers are unlikely to separate Internet shopping from other forms of shopping; in fact, they consider it as a part of their continual purchasing journey and it must meet their shopping needs along with the other channels (Kaufman-Scarborough and Lindquist, 2002; Kwon and Lennon, 2009). It can be argued that a well-structured omnichannel supply chain can be efficient and customer-responsive at the same time if it can capture the main strengths that the brick-and-mortar and online channels can deliver (Chopra, 2016).

Recently, Stolze et al. (2016) pointed out that with the advent of shopper marketing, the issue is no longer one of matching a supply chain to a product; as Fisher (1997) explained, the need is for efficient or responsive supply chain strategies. Instead, marketing and supply chain managers need to ask: 'What is the right supply chain for our shopper?' This is a new challenge for the whole supply chain. For example, e-shoppers are looking for the best delivery choices, higher control and flexible alternatives to home delivery in their relentless search for convenience and a better price. In particular, research results reinforce that most shoppers are looking for the best deal on shipping. In a research study (Ganesh and Engleson, 2016), two-day delivery preference was shown to be rising over the last two years (20% in 2016 v. 16% in 2015 and 10% in 2014), while 69% of participants expected options three to five days from time of purchase to delivery. Amazon Prime is likely driving this increase as members select two-day shipping 31% of the time, on average, compared with an average of only 8% for non-members. In addition, Amazon (see box 3.1) is just at the beginning of investing in a brick and mortar store. The company might also use stores as pick-up points for online purchases completely unrelated to groceries. It will be a good combination between the convenience of online ordering

---

Box 3.1   Amazon Fresh and Amazon Go

Usually, there is an evolution from offline to online stores, so brick-and-mortar stores go digital. However, being in an omnichannel context can also mean the opposite. For instance, pure e-tailers may face the need to go offline. In the case of Amazon, *The Wall Street Journal* states that this giant e-tailer will open new stores offline for fresh food that consumers will order online. The Seattle company aims to build brick-and-mortar stores that will sell produce such as milk, meats and other perishable items that customers can take home. Primarily using their mobile phones or, possibly, touchscreens in the store, customers could also order other goods with longer shelf lives for same-day delivery. For customers seeking a quicker checkout, Amazon will soon design and develop drive-in locations where online grocery orders could be brought to the car (Bensinger and Tevens, 2016) In addition, with the newest project called Amazon Go, shopping will become easier with checkout-free shopping.

Such experience is made possible by the same types of technologies used in self-driving cars: computer vision, sensor fusion and deep learning. This technology automatically detects when products are taken from or returned to the shelves and keeps track of them in a virtual cart. When consumers have finished their shopping, they can exit the store and they will be charged through their Amazon account. The requirements are to have an Amazon account, a supported smartphone and the free Amazon Go app. Amazon Go is in its beta format in the only open store for employees in Seattle, but it will open in 2017 to the public and the plan is to replicate such experience in other new stores (www.amazon.com/b?node=16008589011).

with the ability to choose some items like food, meat, fish and vegetables in the store. Amazon is definitely trying to build an innovative business model where logistics plays a key role.

Having an online presence is not only a priority for 'pure' e-tailers. For instance, large retailers who have been operating for decades in the brick-and-mortar market are likely to exploit the effect of digitalisation, bringing their positive perception of the offline brand to the online one. This is confirmed by previous research, which found that consumers are likely to trust well-known retailers more than new retailers that are only present on the Internet (Kwon and Lennon, 2009). At the same time, consumers can benefit through online discounts, coupons and other advantages when going offline to buy. Particularly in Asian markets, consumers are likely to use many of the in-store digital enablement options, as reported in a recent survey by Nielsen (illustrated in Figure 3.1). This trend is lower in Latin America, but the willingness to try them in the future is higher. The same is true for European consumers, who might try such in-store tools in the future. Considering the main digital engagement options, the most used are online or mobile coupons (16.6%), followed by login to the in-store Wi-Fi to receive more information (11%). Moreover, almost 52.6% of respondents of Nielsen survey are willing to use coupons in the future, while 64.4 % will login to the Wi-Fi store. Other digital tools that are adopted by consumers in-store are retailers' apps on mobile phones or scanning QR code. All of these tools aim at receiving information and offers about products. The same works for in-store computers or quick response (QR) codes through which consumers can search for information about product assortment and access more information about discounts, offers or prices. All numbers related to the adoption of these tools are reported in Figure 3.1.

To summarise, this integration between offline and online retail has led to a significant change both to companies' operations management and to the market structure (Nicholson, Clarke and Blakemore, 2002). Doubtless, the multichannel approach helps companies to reach and maintain customer loyalty better through the increase of customer touchpoints, providing customers with more channels and different types of products, and service offerings (Cassab and MacLachlan, 2006). In addition, such integration represents an improvement in a customer's experience with the companies, as she or he has multiple options to contact and to communication with the brand, strengthen her or his brand attachment and reinforce her or his retention to the brand (Gefen, 2000; Harvin, 2000; Bailer, 2006). Such benefits can be reached by companies only if its offline reputation is positive, because when customers have a negative experience with a brand in one channel, this can impact the perception they have of the same brand in another channel. Succeeding online implies to be able to design and implement an accurate strategy to be satisfactory in all channels offering what customer need. The key role is played by planning an integrated approach, which considers the channels all together within a common strategy.

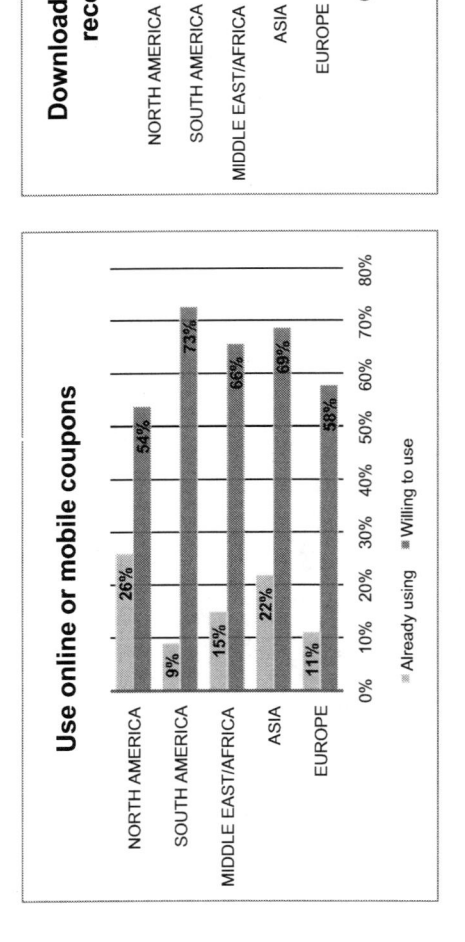

Use online or mobile coupons

NORTH AMERICA — Already using 26%, Willing to use 54%
SOUTH AMERICA — Already using 9%, Willing to use 73%
MIDDLE EAST/AFRICA — Already using 15%, Willing to use 66%
ASIA — Already using 22%, Willing to use 69%
EUROPE — Already using 11%, Willing to use 58%

Already using   Willing to use

Download retailer app or mobile phone to receive information or offers

NORTH AMERICA — Already using 15%, Willing to use 51%
SOUTH AMERICA — Already using 8%, Willing to use 72%
MIDDLE EAST/AFRICA — Already using 13%, Willing to use 68%
ASIA — Already using 18%, Willing to use 68%
EUROPE — Already using 7%, Willing to use 53%

Already using   Willing to use

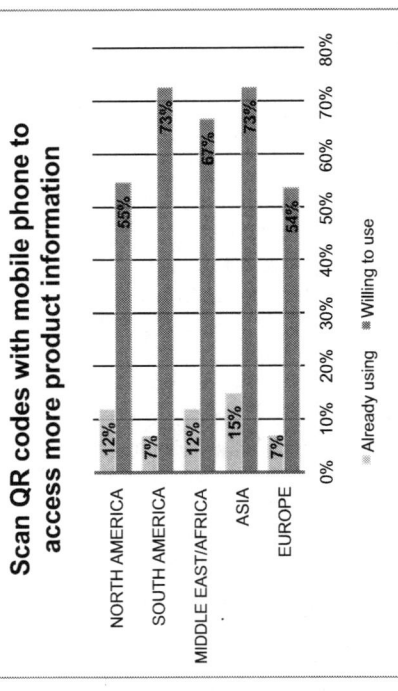

Login to wifi in-store with their mobile to receive information and offers

NORTH AMERICA — Already using 12%, Willing to use 54%
SOUTH AMERICA — Already using 9%, Willing to use 73%
MIDDLE EAST/AFRICA — Already using 14%, Willing to use 68%
ASIA — Already using 15%, Willing to use 72%
EUROPE — Already using 5%, Willing to use 55%

Already using   Willing to use

Scan QR codes with mobile phone to access more product information

NORTH AMERICA — Already using 12%, Willing to use 55%
SOUTH AMERICA — Already using 7%, Willing to use 73%
MIDDLE EAST/AFRICA — Already using 12%, Willing to use 67%
ASIA — Already using 15%, Willing to use 73%
EUROPE — Already using 7%, Willing to use 54%

Already using   Willing to use

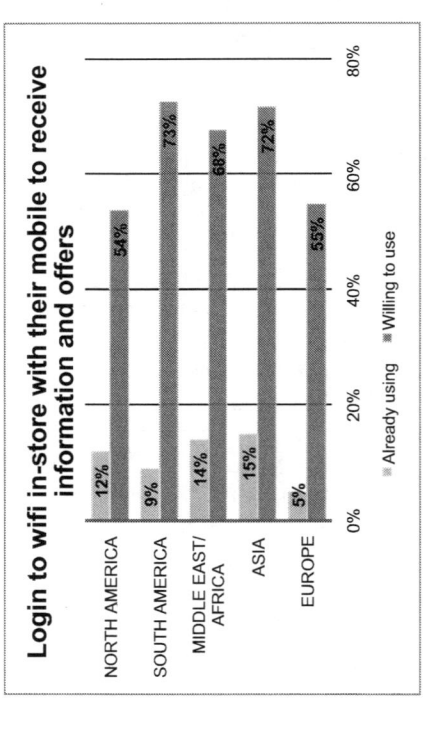

Figure 3.1 In-store digital enablement adoption

Source: Adapted from Nielsen (2015) www.nielsen.com/us/en/insights/news/2015/savvy-in-store-solutions-drive-digital-minded-consumers.html

B2B digital transformation and requirements

> The CEO of a major supplier to the telecom industry was frustrated. An initiative to increase sales volumes and shift the company's product mix to higher-value components was stalling, and not for lack of effort. With support from a marketing campaign that emphasised a slew of new product features, frontline sales managers had stepped up calls to their purchasing contacts at Original Equipment Manufacturer customers. Yet they reported that buyers weren't buying. Impediments appeared to include tough new requirements from chief purchasing officers, negative chatter on social media about post-sales support, and sceptical questions on a product-rating site about an offering's fully loaded costs.
>
> (Lingqvist, Plotkin and Stanley, 2015)

This is a new scenario that many companies are also facing in the B2B context. Digitalisation has not only changed customers' purchasing behaviour and habits but it has of course provided companies with consistent new opportunities and challenges. This implies a rethink, not only about what they offer to final consumers but also about changes in their organisation, skills and activities. Within this context, B2B companies need to adjust accordingly. It means a great effort in organisational, operational and technological aspects must take place to allow this digital evolution and a cross-functional collaboration among partners (Yan, 2011). A recent survey by Accenture (Brozek, 2015) found that B2B firms are striving to develop their digital skills but are 'far from achieving digital mastery'. Indubitably, the advent of the digital environment has improved and supports traditional marketing in the B2B context, although companies are still meeting some problems in integration among channels, providing the right content in the right place and pursuing marketing objectives in the right channel. This is truer for small and medium enterprise firms, whose selling models are tightly anchored in the offline word, while activities in the online channels often represent little more than having a company website that acts as a digital brochure and does not provide customers the opportunity to buy or to interact with the company.

According to Järvinen, Tollinen, Karjaluoto and Jayawardhena (2012) and Karjaluoto, Mustonen and Ulkuniemi (2015), digitalisation can help to achieve several aims in the B2B sector. These can be summarised as follows:

- cost reductions achieved through an improvement of efficiency of communications and transactions,
- better provision of brand and product-related information that helps companies to create awareness, brand attitude, and increasing purchase intentions,
- sales increase through facilitation of transaction processes and driving traffic to a company website,
- new platform creations that help companies to improve interaction and relationship with and among customers,
- access to a massive range of digital tools that can be used for marketing purposes and improving communication,
- access to huge amount of data about customers, customers' journey, competitors, products that can be useful for marketing purposes,

- content creation thanks to customers who become participants and active content creators in the communication process.

(Hennig-Thurau et al., 2010)

Above all, what digitalisation has provided to everyone is the opportunity to express their opinion, to share ideas, provide reviews and help other people to make a better choice. This has led people to trust their peers more than companies (Karjaluoto et al., 2015). This change also has several implications for B2B companies, which need to learn and be more involved in understanding and listening to customers. Particularly online, the role of companies is to provide a fertile context that allows customers to collaborate and participate in communities. A challenge for B2B companies is to combine and integrate offline and online communication with the common aim of creating more value. The first action to take is to learn how to use these channels and how the use will affect the buyer-seller relationship (Parasuraman and Zinkhan, 2002; Day and Bens, 2005; Constantinides and Fountain, 2008; Hennig-Thurau et al., 2010; Kerrigan and Graham, 2010; Michaelidou, Siamagka and Christodoulides, 2011; Järvinen et al., 2012) The two most important pillars for this context are interactivity and content. Interactivity implies the need to have bidirectional communication between sellers and buyers, while content is related to the need for companies to publish interesting content to help customers in their purchasing process, which must be easy to access in the different channels. Social media perfectly fits this role of providing interactivity and meaningful content. Usually, social media topics are better explored in the B2C context, both from academic and managerial perspectives. However, social media can be helpful in the B2B context by providing companies with the opportunity to generate viral effects and positive WOM (Mangold and Faulds, 2009; Hanna, Rohm and Crittenden, 2011). Nevertheless, having fewer customers and being less willing to generate viral effects, B2B companies may decide to utilise social media to reach other goals: foremost to drive more traffic to their website, to optimise search engines and to provide a better conversation tool for existing customers. Therefore, this can lead to improved customer relationships and better listening to customers' needs, problems and requests. This will enhance satisfaction and loyalty, particularly for large-sized companies (Karjaluoto et al., 2015). Clearly, B2C companies may perceive less efforts for this transformation than B2B companies, as the latter would have to take a more structured approach and exercise more control over their investments in going digital. Some of the benefits derived from digital marketing that are appropriate for B2C settings are not available in industrial marketing settings because of the different norms of communication in customer relationships. For example, open or public discussion with customers in social media can threaten confidentiality and therefore breaks the norms of communication in the industrial business field. B2B companies may not feel willing to provide and allow open communication, as they can perceive this as a threat of losing competitive advantage and customers. Conversely, digital tools can improve efficiency of communication, both internal and external, allowing better information exchange. Another challenge would be dealing with a huge amount of data that the online context provides to companies and its management. Data security has become one of the top risks across all industries and company sizes.

The loss of sensitive data is dangerous also for all companies, including logistics companies, as they can lose competitive advantage through data breaches and through the overexposure of their competitive resources that are promoted and illustrated online to customers. This can lead to a lack of originality and the advent of new competitors that offer similar products or services in a substitute way, leading to a disruption in certain industries. Think, for instance, of transportation with Uber versus the taxi, or of the tourism industry with Airbnb in opposition to traditional hotels, or of Netflix versus video rental. In addition, the increase of data also has some consequences in terms of the new skills, capabilities and tools that are required to manage them. Often, companies lack analytics processes to collect, analyse and manage data that could help them to provide better offers to customers and could raise sales. All these barriers can result from different aspects: from the lack of specific skills, expertise and resources to poorly defined goals in the digital context (Järvinen et al., 2012).

Having a digital brand presence can help B2B companies to be more proactive about customers engaging them, although customers can be very far from companies and so difficult to reach. In addition, providing customers with online communities that are built around their brand enhances the brand image and meaning, thereby improving customer value. Conversely, companies can lose control over their brand, and their reputation is more vulnerable (Gaudenzi, Confente and Christopher, 2015; Holliman and Rowley, 2014). Above all, B2B companies need to plan and enrich their online presence, considering ways to reach a more collaborative approach with partners and customers to improve content and relationships. The subsections that follow describe in detail the areas that companies should improve. Figure 3.2 provides a summary of the areas of improvement.

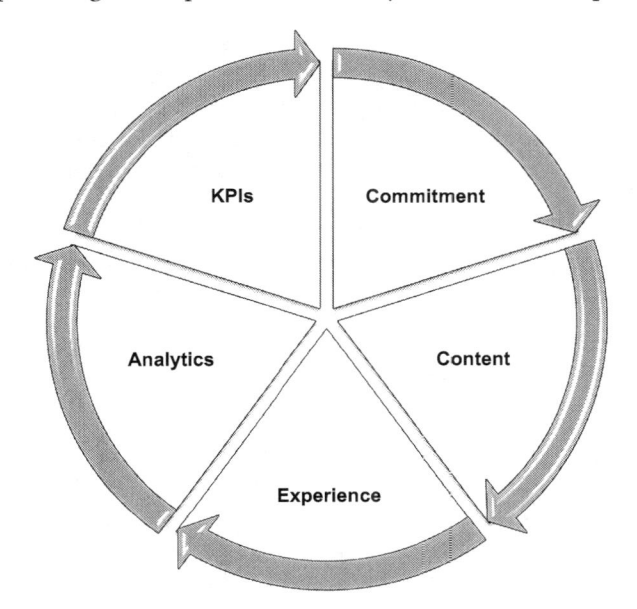

Figure 3.2 Requirements for digital change and success
Source: Our elaboration

Commitment to digital at a strategic level

The first requirement to succeed in the change from being primarily focused on offline activities to the digital shift and transformation is the creation of a culture of innovation within the company. This can help B2B achieve digital success, although almost one-third of B2B companies take more than a year to implement digital initiatives (Catlin, Harrison, Plotkin and Stanley, 2016), and in some cases top management does not share digital objectives with employees. B2B digital leaders, by contrast, underpin agile practices and a widespread culture of collaboration among partners and employees who actively take part in the digital strategy. Such collaboration results in a faster time to market and more effectiveness.

Succeeding in digital marketing also means prioritising such goals for B2B companies by allocating the necessary resources, instead of allocating only a minor role when deciding resource allocation, which is often the case at present. This might be the cause of a lack of success in the digital market, as companies underestimate the investments in it compared with those for traditional channels.

Box 3.2   General Electric

For example, General Electric (GE) made an audacious move, investing more than $1 billion to create a new market for the Industrial Internet. To make its digital strategy the de facto way of operating, GE consolidated each business unit under a chief digital officer (CDO). CDOs report to the chief executive officer (CEO) of the business unit (who in turn reports to the CEO of GE Digital) and have the final say on platform investments. GE also invested more by hiring thousands of new software engineers, user-experience experts and data scientists to acquire specific knowledge and skills. GE's ambitious technology platform now generates $US 5 billion in revenue and the company estimates that business will triple by 2020. A change in the strategic approach needs to reach a shared vision and consensus among management and employees, and it requires new skills and practices on the fly, but it can make a huge difference.

Content

Because of information overload, content and its quality may become one of the most important factors to attract and retain customers. Previous research suggests that beyond the quality of products and services, what is helpful for B2B companies is the concentration on 'soft-selling' through the creation of interesting and helpful digital content (Halligan and Shah, 2009). This involves B2B companies creating and sharing interesting and timely content with customers at the right place and time in their buying decision process. Being at the right place at the right moment with the right information requires organisation and a clear view of customers' journey and decision process. Such results can be obtained through a continuous and interactive engagement with the customers. User-generated content can help B2B companies understand and better explore this phenomenon (Holliman and Rowley, 2014). Among digital content that companies can produce in the digital environment, a recent study has provided the following categories: articles, blogs and micro-blogs, case studies, digital videos and streaming media, e-newsletters, illustrations and graphics, industry events and trade shows, infographics, mobile apps and content, online virtual and immersive environments, product demonstrations, slide decks or presentations, sound bites or comments in social media, supplier comparisons, Web copy (core and microsites), Web interface, Web-based tools and applications, Webinars, as well as white papers, research reports and e-books (Cebglobal, 2012).

Regarding the quality of content, this is defined as the creation of content that helps customers to satisfy a need and to support them in their decision-making process. Such content needs to be interesting and of value (Holliman and Rowley, 2014). This definition is in certain ways similar to the notion of Web-based information quality, which needs to have the following characteristics: usefulness, goodness, accuracy, currency and importance (Rieh, 2002). The content takes place among several players in the B2B context. Among such players, there might exist an overlap of interests and functions that are involved in the content creation. Compared with the B2C context, many industrial players here are involved in the content production.

Experience

According to a recent survey, the top strategic priority for B2B companies is to improve their customers' experience (Brozek, 2015). To reach this goal, more than one-half of respondents stated that they were trying to achieve this aim through the improvement of online experience (58%), across channels (56%) and through call centres (53%). However, compared with B2C companies, B2B firms are still more focused on enhancing traditional touchpoints. Figure 3.3 shows the main actions B2B actors are implementing to augment customer experience compared with B2C companies.

The key to serving the customer better with the ad hoc experience she or he needs to have is to know what the customer's journey is. This allows firms to understand which channels are used for each of the steps consumers adopt to make their purchasing decision. Only in this manner can companies achieve the goal of providing a satisfying experience across channels. This, of course, has some implications, both from marketing and logistics perspectives.

First, B2B companies need to track how each marketing and sales activity adds value to the overall experience. In this way, they can have a footprint of step-by-step experience and the effort they spend for each step, understand which actions has been more effective or which function has been useful. In

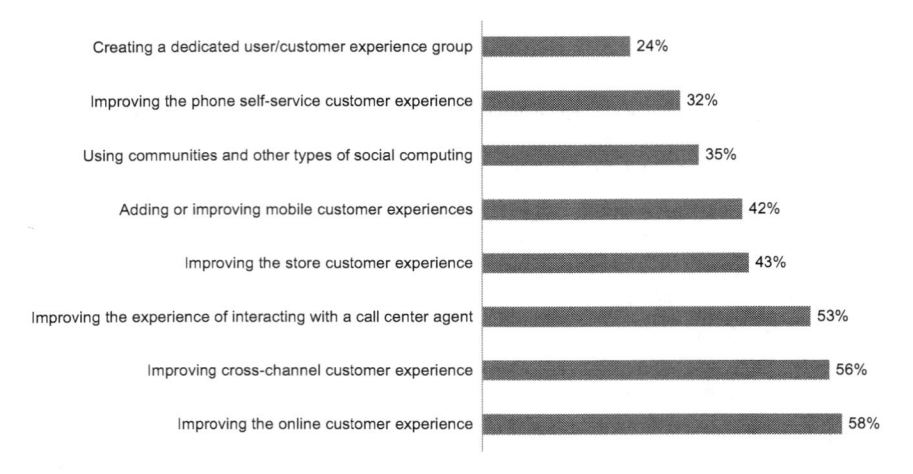

Figure 3.3 Actions to augment customer experience in the B2B context
Source: Adapted from Brozek (2015)

addition, they can identify different types of clients with several buying behaviours and motivations and based on this, and provide them with a tailored experience (Premo, Andersen, Wenstrup and Taneja, 2016). Thus, companies should focus on building long-term and authentic relationships instead of providing customers with time-constrained marketing campaigns. Because B2B firms adopt multiple channels in their purchasing processes, from traditional stores to online websites, they are likely to spend more than single channel buyers. So, being a multichannel – even better, an omnichannel – seller or supplier becomes a priority for B2B companies to increase sales. This has implications also for logistics, and later this will be described in depth. Hence, the big challenge for B2B companies is to avoid selling models that are still working and separate for a single-channel management and to instead integrate channels combing several tools to provide better services and experience to customers.

Data mining and big data analytics

The growth in the quantity and diversity of data has led to data sets larger than are manageable by the conventional hands-on management tools. To manage these new and potentially invaluable data sets, new methods of data science and new applications in the form of predictive analytics have been developed (Russo, Confente and Borghesi, 2015).

The current B2B context is lacking a quasi-real-time feedback from the procurement process itself. Such feedback can help marketing departments of the involved companies exploit corporate comments and ratings that business enterprises post to evaluate the overall improved competitiveness of the value chain. Yet, great care must be exercised in selecting and applying technology within a context as complex as the extended supply chain. Businesses are trying to use automated processes to filter out bad news, understand the topic of the conversations, identify the relevant content and manage it effectively.

This constitutes a huge challenge for B2B companies, which must decide when to go digital and how to collect and manage the huge amount of data they must deal with. A recent study (Stank, Dittmann and Autry, 2011) stated that one of the main pillars in the new supply chain agenda is choosing the right technology for SCM and successfully implementing it to succeed in the market. This is also confirmed in practice, as top-performing B2B firms are using advanced technologies to improve their skills of data analytics and better explore the available data they have about consumers. This helps firms to provide a valuable marketing offering with the right content and the tailored service that customers want.

Customer relationship management systems need to be integrated with data about customers' journeys (in terms of time, channels and actions). Digitalisation might help in this sense to collect systematic information exchange between sales, marketing and logistics. The results will be that the marketing function could assist the sales function by offering materials that meet the customers' needs more completely. In turn, the sales function could be more aware of the need to align sales presentations to customers with the broader strategic marketing objectives of the company (Karjaluoto et al., 2015). Supply chain managers and logistics managers could have more reliable data about demand forecast and better visibility about orders. In addition, companies should invest in 'next-product-to-buy' analytics that recommend to customers the next actions and products they could engage with. This helps companies to increase sales too. Advanced analytics help companies increase sales and manage a more crowded, competitive context. Digital tools that can trigger sales and personal selling can range from mobile devices that facilitate Customer Relationship Management to sales-support material and better display of products. Similar data-enabled marketing practices allow B2B companies to create highly targeted campaigns that help them position their offer in the market better, creating a competitive advantage.

More generally, to maintain a lasting advantage, predicting the customer's next purchase is not enough. Big data can help companies to have a deep understanding about what creates and leads to customer stickiness, loyalty and relationships. The objective for companies should be more focused on what the customer's lifetime value will be than what price she or he will be willing to pay for her or his next purchase (Dawar, 2016). This consideration should deal not merely with marketing and sales campaigns but also reflect the entire company strategy to reach and maintain customers' loyalty. Managing and dealing with large volumes of data of course has implication for logistics and supply chains. Box 3.3 will provide a better explanation of such implications.

Box 3.3   Big data in the supply chain

Competition in the supply chain is based on drivers such as accuracy, speed and quality, which force companies to reach a level that is not possible to reach through traditional enterprise resource planning (ERP) and SCM systems. The depth, scale and scope of data supply chains that have been generating over the last decade are growing fast and require more specialised skills to be able to collect and manage them. Such data, the so-called big data, are unique because of their volume, variety, velocity and veracity, and today are widely available and much less expensive to access and store (McAfee and Brynjolfsson, 2012).

Big data can be collected and analysed thanks to the adoption and integration of several technology platforms (e.g., cloud computing). In addition, only through accurate predictive analytics can companies capture and analyse big data in a real-time context, which can help them to demand better forecast and demand shaping (Ketchen, Crook and Craighead, 2014). Supply chain–related technology already exists, and the benefits of implementing the right technological portfolio can be significant for many firms (Richey, Tokman and Dalela, 2009). However, because of the larger amount of data, supply chains need to collect data across several sources not only inside but outside the supply chain. A recent study reported an overview of the sources from which big data are generated and results found they come from 52 sources of big data that are generated in supply chains (Rozados and Tjahjono, 2014).

In fact, big data comes in different forms from different sources. It can be structured or unstructured. It can be in written form or verbal conversation; it can come from radiofrequency or in the form of a tweet or post (Sanders, 2014). Trying to represent this in a plot, such sources can be classified by variety (less and more), volume and velocity (less and more) plotted by the relative level of structured or unstructured data. Figure 3.4 provides some examples of structured, unstructured and semi-structured data classified based on their volume and velocity.

Predictive analytics can act as a facilitator helping supply chains to collect and manage such large volumes of data. As Waller and Fawcett (2013) stated:

> SCM predictive analytics use both quantitative and qualitative methods to improve supply chain design and competitiveness by estimating past and future levels of integration of business processes among functions or companies, as well as the associated costs and service levels.

(p. 80)

Such analyses help supply chains to estimate past and future levels of integration among processes, functions and companies determining the level of

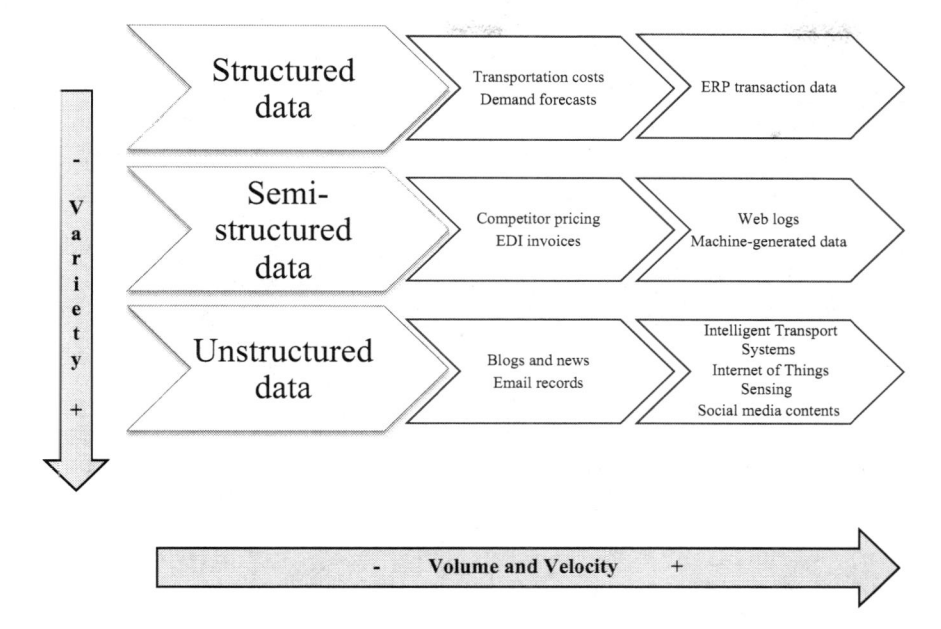

Figure 3.4 SCM data variety, volume and velocity
Source: Adapted from Rozados and Tjahjono (2014).

competitiveness and the related costs and service levels. For this reason, one of the main goals of managers should be to collect and manage data with a high degree of accuracy to ensure data quality. In essence, they should begin to view the quality of the data products they base their decisions on in much the same way they view the quality of the products their supply chain delivers (Hazen et al., 2014). In fact, one threat supply chain managers should be aware of is the poor quality of data, which could become a cost when basing their decisions on them. The increasing importance of data should lead supply chain managers to be more sensitive and aware about collecting and managing high-quality data.

According to Russo et al. (2015) and Waller and Fawcett (2013), big data can have a significant impact on SCM and its processes. For instance, big data management can act as an enabler to improve the procurement process and better predict future demand. In addition, it can facilitate companies to reach a better inventory accuracy, receiving in return a real-time capacity availability and being able to provide a quicker response and vendor-managed inventory.

Big data have the potential to provide improved traceability performance and reduce the thousands of hours lost just trying to access, integrate and manage product databases that provide data on where products are in the field that need to be recalled or retrofitted.

Lastly, big data management can optimise logistics activities thanks to costs reduction, improved customer satisfaction and supply chain performance. This is also confirmed by a recent study by Richey Jr et al. (2016), which found that managers perceive the following key success factors of big data use: better decision-making, operational efficiency, data security, adequate storage and transparency in partnerships to provide and consume big data. One of the big challenges for long global supply chains is to capture data at multiple points, both internal and external, to improve the customer experience. Linking big data and supply chain dynamics in a B2B context represents a terrific opportunity for future research. This would specifically take into consideration the areas of procurement, inventory management and logistics management, making an effort to provide examples of potential applications of big data to logistics and SCM practice. Table 3.2 attempts to define this at a conceptual level. Each row represents a different member of the supply chain (carrier, manufacturer as a supplier, retailer) combined with three different columns of potential supply chain area, of application and of big data. All the implications have in common the predictive nature, thanks to an improvement in information sharing. This is not intended to be an exhaustive list and it might be further enriched and integrated. In addition, there might be some overlapping across users for the same category.

So, for example at the level of procurement strategy, managing big data means analysing all the data from retailers, carriers, manufacturers and suppliers, as well

Table 3.2 Examples of potential applications of big data at procurement level

Role	Procurement
Carrier	Time of delivery, factoring in weather, driver characteristics, time of day and date to supply the manufacturers.
Manufacturer	Better prediction of future demand; easier response to the need of spend information, integration of data with carriers and retailers, reduced order-to-delivery cycle times.
Retailer	Use of mobile devices in stores to manage the replenishment system; vendor-managed inventory.

Source: Adapted from Waller and Fawcett (2013)

Table 3.3 Examples of potential applications of big data at inventory management level

Role	Inventory management
Carrier	Real-time capacity availability.
Manufacturer	Reduction in shrink, efficient consumer response, quick response; vendor-managed inventory, inventory repositioned.
Retailer	Improvement in perpetual inventory system accuracy (better stock management).

Source: Adapted from Waller and Fawcett (2013)

as from external events linking with a firm's own business (e.g., traffic congestions, weather, road constraints); this allows visibility. From a buyer's perspective, the data visibility through analysing product assortments from major suppliers in real time can offer an on-time picture of the products in stock and their availability; moreover, it helps to manage dynamically the deal prices on the base of competitors' prices, demand conditions, seasons and other external conditions. Sharing data with the buyers allows suppliers to understand what and when they want products and to assess the level of service.

At an inventory management level, effective big data management would help companies to achieve a real-time capacity availability and this would provide a quicker response and vendor-managed inventory. In addition, providing supply chain managers with real-time data would help to reduce shrinkage and enable a more efficient consumer response. Conversely, retailers could benefit from big data analysis to improve their inventory accuracy, updating their sales and their product availability located in different stores and warehouses

Moreover, the flow of information in this process is slow and costly and the process is not being executed efficiently. Automatic analysis of data from sources such as mobile equipment, sensor networks and geospatial devices can significantly improve the accuracy of SCM transportation processes. This contributes to supply chain performance by minimising delivery attempts and ensuring higher customer satisfaction, as deliveries are carried out when customers can receive them. For instance, huge amounts of data are being generated by truckers using smartphones at very limited costs; firms could utilise their location data to provide real-time speed maps of the entire roadway system, as well to identify accidents, congestions or incidents.

Generally, efficient and effective big data analytics could help manufacturers to reduce costs adopting a real-time approach.

For the manufacturer or supplier, ensuring customer satisfaction, and later customer loyalty, is a key goal of their supply chain strategy However, a customer's

Table 3.4 Examples of potential applications of big data at logistics management

Role	Logistics management
Carrier	Optimal routing, taking into account weather, traffic congestion and driver characteristics; substitution of transport and logistics documentation with real-time information through mobile devices, enhancing level of service.
Manufacturer	Improved notification of delivery time and availability; surveillance data for improved yard management; improved level of customer service.
Retailer	Linking local traffic congestion and weather to store traffic; coordination of transportation processes with other supply chain players.

Source: Adapted from Waller and Fawcett (2013)

orientation in a supply chain represents a far more complex issue than managing customer loyalty within a single firm, even as it offers the potential for increased benefits to participant firms in terms of profitability.

In fact, despite the difficulties companies face collecting, managing and interpreting large volumes of data, the impact of big data on revolutionising SCM is a matter of fact. According to a recent report of SCM World (2014), 64% of supply chain executives consider big data analytics a disruptive and important technology, setting the foundation for long-term change management in their companies. However, this requires cross-functional integration and cross-company human-technology interface aspects that can add a much higher dimension of complexity to adoption, acceptance and usage decisions

Such technology enables a better sharing and collaboration among members of the network, adding value that goes beyond the mere transaction. This latter is not the main goal but, instead, creating knowledge-sharing networks can be achieved from big data analytics. Collaboration and visibility among processes and companies allows supply chains to gain several results: to improve customer service and fulfilment, to react faster to supply chain issues, to increase efficiency and to improve integration.

To summarise, while many companies are adopting big data to create new forms of value, other companies are still far from adopting it to revolutionise their supply chain operations (Sanders, 2016). To be a successful instrument, it requires that members of the supply chain networks have the right degree of connectivity and information sharing, as well as top management commitment in big data analytics (Gunasekaran et al., 2017).

Measuring digital impact through key performance indicators

Last but not least, another activity that B2B companies need to implement and perfect is to control their presence and performance across channels through ad hoc metrics and the development of appropriate dashboards of key performance indicators (KPIs). This implies the adoption of the right technology and the definition and implementation of KPIs that are enabled to align company objectives with the digital context. In turn, this means understanding the degree of customer relationship building and maintenance, providing companies with real-time feedback about their online activities in terms of customer engagement, acquisition and lifetime, plus the development of KPIs related to companies' performance in terms of order management and fulfilment, order accuracy, delivery time and returns rates. Compared with the offline context, digital activities are easier to measure as they are more visible and traceable (Hennig-Thurau et al., 2010). However, because of the larger amount of data and information to track and control, there is a need for companies to adopt automated data collection and analysis (Pauwels et al., 2009). Consequently, companies are in a better position to measure their online presence and performance in the digital channel, and this activity can be improved by adopting two key digital solutions – Web analytics (WA) and social media monitoring (SMM) software (Järvinen et al., 2012).

The first tool enables companies to track customers' behaviour within the company website by monitoring click-stream data to understand the volume of traffic generation and customers' journeys in terms of evaluation of products, information collection through downloading of materials such as brochures and special offers and the decision to purchase or to abandon the website (Wilson, 2010). WA allows firms to monitor specific digital marketing campaigns as well understand what consumers are paying attention to, or not paying attention to, in order to improve their websites. They can also match customers' online journey with their personal data if they are registered, or subscribe to their website, suggesting to them ad hoc and precise marketing actions.

To integrate data collection and analysis of online activities, the second important tool is SMM, which helps companies to integrate information about digital conversations that flow into social media platforms. Such platforms represent a fertile context where discussions about products, services and brands proliferate. Tracking and collecting such conversations allows firms to gain benefits for B2B companies also. However, such an ability is still under-exploited by B2B firms and digital measurement and technology adoption is still limited. This shift from offline to online has certain implications, not only from a marketing perspective but also from the perspective of logistics and SCM. The next chapter will explain this perspective.

Note

1 Industry 4.0 focuses on the end-to-end digitisation of all physical assets and integration into digital ecosystems with value chain partners.

References

Bailer, C. (2006) 'Stocking the customer experience', *CRM Magazine*, 10(9), 15.

Bensinger, G. and Stevens, L. (2016) *Amazon to expand grocery business with new convenience stores*. Available at www.wsj.com/articles/amazon-to-expand-grocery-business-with-new-convenience-stores-1476189657. Accessed on 28th December 2016.

Brozek, M. (2015) *Digital transformation in the age of the customer*. Available at www.accenture.com/_acnmedia/Accenture/Conversion-Assets/DotCom/Documents/Global/PDF/Digital_1/Accenture-Digital-Transformation-B2B-spotlight.pdf. Accessed on 20th November 2016.

Cassab, H. and MacLachlan, D. L. (2006) 'Interaction fluency: a customer performance measure of multichannel service', *International Journal of Productivity and Performance Management*, 55(7), 555–568.

Catlin, T., Harrison, L., Plotkin, C. L. and Stanley, J. (2016) *How B2B digital leaders drive five times more revenue growth than their peers*. Available at www.mckinsey.com/business-functions/marketing-and-sales/our-insights/how-b2b-digital-leaders-drive-five-times-more-revenue-growth-than-their-peers?cid=other-eml-alt-mip-mck-oth-1610. Accessed on 22nd October 2016.

CEB Marketing Leadership Council. (2012) *The digital evolution in B2B marketing*. Available at www.cebglobal.com/content/dam/cebglobal/us/EN/best-practices-decision-support/marketing-communications/pdfs/CEB-Mktg-B2B-Digital-Evolution.pdf. Accessed on 22nd October 2016.

Chopra, S. (2016) 'How omni-channel can be the future of retailing', *Decision*, 43(2), 135–144.

Christopher, M. and Holweg, M. (2011) '"Supply chain 2.0": managing supply chains in the era of turbulence', *International Journal of Physical Distribution & Logistics Management*, 41(1), 63–82.

Constantinides, E. and Fountain, S. J. (2008) 'Web 2.0: conceptual foundations and marketing issues', *Journal of Direct, Data and Digital Marketing Practice*, 9(3), 231–244.

Cummins, S., Peltier, J. W. and Dixon, A. (2016) 'Omni-channel research framework in the context of personal selling and sales management', *Journal of Research in Interactive Marketing*, 10(1), 2–16.

Dawar, N. (2016) 'Use big data to create value for customers, not just target them', *Harvard Business Review*, October 2016. Available at https://hbr.org/2016/08/use-big-data-to-create-value-for-customers-not-just-target-them. Accessed on 14th January 2017.

Day, G. and Bens, K. (2005) 'Capitalizing on the internet opportunity', *Journal of Business & Industrial Marketing*, 20(4/5), 160–168.

Escobar-Rodríguez, T. and Carvajal-Trujillo, E. (2013) 'Online drivers of consumer purchase of website airline tickets', *Journal of Air Transport Management*, 32, 58–64.

Fisher, M. L. (1997) 'What is the right supply I chain for your product?', *Harvard Business Review*, March–April, 1–11.

Forsythe, S., Liu, C., Shannon, D. and Gardner, L. C. (2006) 'Development of a scale to measure the perceived benefits and risks of online shopping', *Journal of Interactive Marketing*, 20(2), 55–75.

Ganesh, B. and Engleson, S. (2016) *UPS pulse of the online shopper*. Available at https://solvers.ups.com/assets/UPS_Pulse_of_the_Online_Shopper.pdf. Accessed on 14th January 2017.

Gaudenzi, B., Confente, I. and Christopher, M. (2015) 'Managing reputational risk: insights from an European survey', *Corporate Reputation Review*, 18(4), 248–260.

Gefen, D. (2000) 'E-commerce: the role of familiarity and trust', *Omega: The International Journal of Management Science*, 28(6), 725–737.

Gunasekaran, A., Papadopoulos, T., Dubey, R., Wamba, S. F., Childe, S. J., Hazen, B. and Akter, S. (2017) 'Big data and predictive analytics for supply chain and organizational performance', *Journal of Business Research*, 70, 308–317.

Halligan, B. and Shah, D. (2009) *Inbound marketing: get found using Google, social media, and blogs*. New York: John Wiley & Sons.

Hanna, R., Rohm, A. and Crittenden, V. L. (2011) 'We're all connected: the power of the social media ecosystem', *Business Horizons*, 54(3), 265–273.

Harvin, R. (2000) 'In Internet branding, the off-lines have it', *Brandweek*, 41(4), 30–31.

Hazen, B. T., Boone, C. A., Ezell, J. D. and Jones-Farmer, L. A. (2014) 'Data quality for data science, predictive analytics, and big data in supply chain management: an introduction to the problem and suggestions for research and applications', *International Journal of Production Economics*, 154, 72–80.

Hennig-Thurau, T., Malthouse, E. C., Friege, C., Gensler, S., Lobschat, L., Rangaswamy, A. and Skiera, B. (2010) 'The impact of new media on customer relationships', *Journal of Service Research*, 13(3), 311–330.

Holliman, G. and Rowley, J. (2014) 'Business to business digital content marketing: marketers' perceptions of best practice', *Journal of Research in Interactive Marketing*, 8(4), 269–293.

Hsin Chang, H., Tsai, Y.-C. and Hsu, C.-H. (2013) 'E-procurement and supply chain performance', *Supply Chain Management: An International Journal*, 18(1), 34–51.

Järvinen, J., Tollinen, A., Karjaluoto, H. and Jayawardhena, C. (2012) 'Digital and social media marketing usage in B2B industrial section', *Marketing Management Journal*, 22(2), 102–117.

Jiang, L., Yang, Z. and Jun, M. (2013) 'Measuring consumer perceptions of online shopping convenience', *Journal of Service Management*, 24(2), 191–214.

Karjaluoto, H., Mustonen, N. and Ulkuniemi, P. (2015) 'The role of digital channels in industrial marketing communications', *Journal of Business & Industrial Marketing*, 30(6), 703–710.

Kaufman-Scarborough, C. and Lindquist, J. D. (2002) 'E-shopping in a multiple channel environment', *Journal of Consumer Marketing*, 19(4), 333–350.

Kerrigan, F. and Graham, G. (2010) 'Interaction of regional news-media production and consumption through the social space', *Journal of Marketing Management*, 26(3/4), 302–320.

Ketchen, D. J., Crook, T. R. and Craighead, C. W. (2014) 'From supply chains to supply ecosystems: implications for strategic sourcing research and practice', *Journal of Business Logistics*, 35(3), 165–171.

Khurana, A. and Al-Olama, B. S. (2016) *Industry 4.0: building the digital industrial enterprise*. Available at www.pwc.com/m1/en/publications/documents/middle-east-industry-4-0-survey.pdf. Accessed on 8th January 2017.

Kushwaha, T. and Shankar, V. (2013) 'Are multichannel customers really more valuable? the moderating role of product category characteristics', *Journal of Marketing*, 77(4), 67–85.

Kwon, W. S. and Lennon, S. J. (2009) 'What induces online loyalty? Online versus offline brand images', *Journal of Business Research*, 62(5), 557–564.

Lingqvist, O., Plotkin, C. L. and Stanley, J. (2015) *Do you really understand how your business customers buy?* Available at www.mckinsey.com/business-functions/marketing-and-sales/our-insights/do-you-really-understand-how-your-business-customers-buy. Accessed on 8th January 2017.

Lusch, R. F. and Vargo, S. L. (2014) The service-dominant logic of marketing: dialog, debate, and directions, New York: Routledge.

Mangold, W. G. and Faulds, D. J. (2009) 'Social media: the new hybrid element of the promotion mix', *Business Horizons*, 52(4), 357–365.

McAfee, A. P (2006) 'Enterprise 2.0: the dawn of emergent collaboration', *MIT Sloan Management Review*, 47(3), 21–28.

McAfee, A. P. and Brynjolfsson, E. (2012) 'Big data: the management revolution', *Harvard Business Review*, 90(10), 60–68.

Michaelidou, N., Siamagka, N. T. and Christodoulides, G. (2011) 'Usage, barriers and measurement of social media marketing: an exploratory investigation of small and medium B2B brands', *Industrial Marketing Management*, 40(7), 1153–1159.

Nicholson, M., Clarke, I. and Blakemore, M. (2002) '"One brand, three ways to shop": situational variables and multichannel consumer behaviour', *The International Review of Retail, Distribution and Consumer Research*, 12(2), 131–148.

Nielsen. (2015) *Savvy in-store solutions drive digital-minded consumers*. Available at www.nielsen.com/us/en/insights/news/2015/savvy-in-store-solutions-drive-digital-minded-consumers.html. Accessed on 17th November 2016.

Nielsen. (2016) *Global connected commerce*. Available at www.nielsen.com/content/dam/corporate/us/en/reports-downloads/2016-reports/connected-commerce-report-jan-2016.pdf. Accessed on 17th November 2016.

Parasuraman, A. and Zinkhan, G. (2002) 'Marketing to and serving customers through the internet: an overview and research agenda', *Journal of the Academy of Marketing Science*, 30(4), 286–295.

Pauwels, K., Ambler, T., Clark, B. H., LaPointe, P., Reibstein, D., Skiera, B. and Wierenga, B. (2009) 'Dashboards as a service: why, what, how, and what research is needed?', *Journal of Service Research*, 12(2), 175–189.

Premo, R., Andersen, P., Wenstrup, J. and Taneja, V. (2016) *Five selling secrets of today's digital B2B leaders*. Available at www.bcgperspectives.com/content/articles/sales-channels-marketing-sales-five-selling-secrets-todays-digital-b2b-leaders/.

Quiring, K. and Schunck, O. (2015) *Is digital killing loyalty?* Available at www.accenture.com/t20160914T055657__w__/us-en/_acnmedia/Accenture/Conversion-Assets/DotCom/Documents/Global/PDF/Dualpub_13/Accenture-Is-Digital-Killing-Loyalty.pdf#zoom=50. Accessed on 17th October 2016.

Rangaswamy, A. and Van Bruggen, G. H. (2005) 'Opportunities and challenges in multichannel marketing: an introduction to the special issue', *Journal of Interactive Marketing*, 19(2), 5–11.

Richey Jr., R. G., Morgan, T. R., Lindsey-Hall, K. and Adams, F. G. (2016) 'A global exploration of big data in the supply chain', *International Journal of Physical Distribution & Logistics Management*, 46(8), 710–739.

Richey, R. G., Tokman, M. and Dalela, V. (2009) 'Examining collaborative supply chain service technologies: a study of intensity, relationships, and resources', *Journal of the Academy of Marketing Science*, 38(1), 71–89.

Rieh, S. Y. (2002) Judgment of information quality and cognitive authority in the Web. *Journal of the American Society for Information Science and Technology*, 53(2), 145–161.

Rozados, I. V. and Tjahjono, B. (2014) *Big data analytics in supply chain management: trends and related research*. Paper Presented at the 6th International Conference on Operations and Supply Chain Management.

Russo, I., Confente, I. and Borghesi, A. (September 2015) *Using big data in the supply chain context: opportunities and challenges*. Paper presented at the European Conference on Knowledge Management, p. 649.

Sanders, N. R. (2014) Big data driven supply chain management: a framework for implementing analytics and turning information into intelligence, Old Tappan, NJ: Pearson Education.

Sanders, N. R. (2016) 'How to use big data to drive your supply chain', *California Management Review*, 58(3), 26–48.

SCM World. (2014) *'Latest chief supply chain officer report' The chief supply chain officer report 2014'*. Available at www.scmworld.com/home/. Accessed on 17th November 2016.

Stank, T. P., Dittmann, P. J. and Autry, C. W. (2011) 'The new supply chain agenda: a synopsis and directions for future research', *International Journal of Physical Distribution & Logistics Management*, 41(10), 940–955.

Stolze, H. J., Mollenkopf, D. A. and Flint, D. J. (2016) 'What is the right supply chain for your shopper? Exploring the shopper service ecosystem', *Journal of Business Logistics*, 37(2), 185–197.

Ternstrand, C., Selldin, E., Virta, N. and Linder, S. (2015) 'Omni-channel retail: a Deloitte point of view.' Available at httpshttps://www2.deloitte.com/content/dam/Deloitte/se/Documents/technology/Omni-channel-2015.pdf. Accessed on 20th January 2017.

Waller, M. A. and Fawcett, S. E. (2013) 'Data science, predictive analytics, and big data: a revolution that will transform supply chain design and management', *Journal of Business Logistics*, 34(2), 77–84.

Wilson, R. D. (2010) 'Using clickstream data to enhance business-to-business web site performance', *Journal of Business & Industrial Marketing*, 25(3), 177–187.

www.accenture.com/t20160914T055657__w__/us-en/_acnmedia/Accenture/Conversion-Assets/DotCom/Documents/Global/PDF/Dualpub_13/Accenture-Is-Digital-Killing-Loyalty.pdf#zoom=50. Accessed on 14th January 2017.

www.amazon.com/b?node=16008589011 (www.amazon.com/b?node=16008589011). Accessed on 14th January 2017.

www.internetlivestats.com/Internet-users/. Accessed on 13rd December 2016.

Yan, R. (2011) 'Managing channel coordination in a multi-channel manufacturer – retailer supply chain', *Industrial Marketing Management*, 40(4), 636–642.

4 Managing the supply chain in the digital context

New issues for supply chain operations

Going digital by integrating traditional channels with digital channels represents a challenge for companies, since this change has several implications for logistics, distribution, organisation management and for the whole supply chain. As an example, Toys "R" Us Inc. prepared for November and December 2016 its entire supply chain of 870 stores to ship nearly twice as many units from its stores. It used inventory in stores for Web orders and organised transport from nearly 25% more from fulfilment centres to serve the Web orders during the Christmas holiday, a period that generates half of all annual toy sales. Moreover, the companies needed to recruit seasonal warehouse workers and keep a balance between online promotions and the ability to fulfil orders quickly, so that items would arrive by Christmas (Ziobro, 2016).

For example, today, major companies must engage in the tentative building of omnichannel strategies as a competitive necessity. They further noted that more research is needed to understand how profits can be yielded from the provision of such services (Goldsby and Zinn, 2016). One of the key issues in this research area is how new channels can be developed by insourcing or outsourcing strategies, how specific resources should be allocated and how operations should be organised across the supply chain. Such practices have changed the rules of competition and raised questions such as: Who controls orders? Who is responsible for pilot delivery lead times? What kind of capabilities does the company need? Who checks the availability of products? What is the role of 3PL? Who manages the reverse logistics in a supply chain network? How firms can reduce supply chain risks?

Continual non-availability of key items could be a major factor in diminishing customer loyalty. Although omnichannel strategy is becoming a competitive necessity, channel integration is hard to achieve, as several companies (most of them at a retail stage) still think separately. In fact, most multichannel retailers maintain a silo structure, where online and offline stores are kept and managed independently of each other (Herhausen, Binder, Schoegel and Herrmann, 2015). Hence, further work remains to be done to achieve channel integration, and this goal remains one of the key focuses for retailers and channel managers.

Integration can enhance customer value perception and from a company perspective can lead to optimised resources and effort, thereby improving efficiency. Of course, there might be a counter-effect of integration: it could be seen as a zero-sum game, creating a sort of cannibalisation among channels (Falk, Schepers, Hammerschmidt and Bauer, 2007) or missing complementarity among distribution channels (Zhang et al., 2010). However, a recent study provides support for the omnichannel, finding no negative effect of omnichannels for traditional stores in terms of cannibalisation or concerning 'channel substitution'. Indeed, authors found support that the Internet channel complements the physical channel (Herhausen et al., 2015). So, achieving channel integration might present advantages but also some threats to companies, and for this reason a deeper analysis of the consequences and implications of omnichannels for each step of the logistics process can be relevant for both academics and practitioners.

The supply chain plays a key role within this context, as it represents the backbone on which online and offline operations take place and are designed. SCM ensures that all processes perform well, that warehousing and distribution operations are optimised and that, at the end, final consumers receive what they have been promised. To close the loop, product returns management represents an increasing challenge for companies because they are a cost driver from one point of view, but they are also a perceived benefit of customers from another point of view. This is, particularly so in the online context where they lower the perceived risk when purchasing online. To gain and maintain a competitive advantage, SCM needs to achieve internal efficiency, reduce costs and at the same time speed the delivery to the final customer, thereby improving effectiveness. To fulfil omnichannel customers' orders, companies must offer

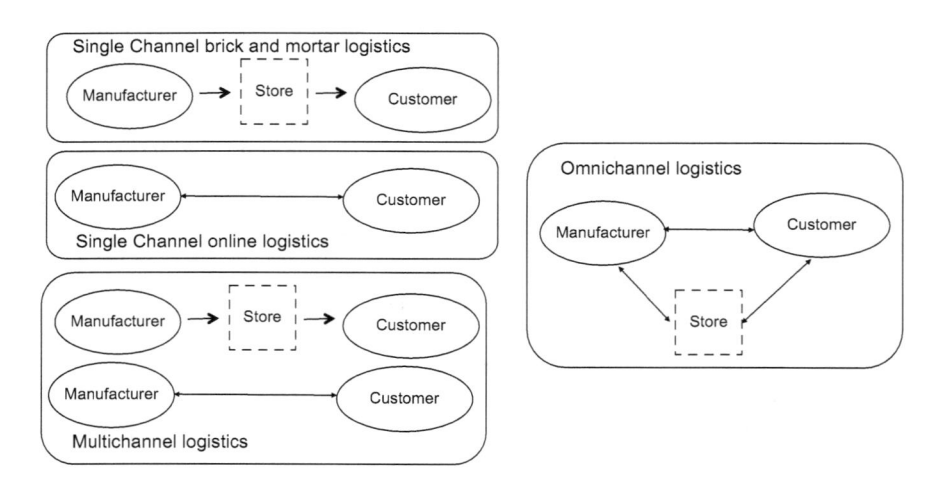

Figure 4.1 Differences between single, multiple and omnichannel logistics

Source: Adapted from Hübner, Holzapfel and Kuhn (2015)

what they want, when they want, where they want. This has serious implications for logistics operations and order fulfilment. To add more complexity, this should be done within two contexts – offline and online – but with orders that come from multiple points: brick and mortar, showrooms, online channels and mobile, among others (Ternstrand, Selldin, Virta and Linder, 2015). Recently, Peinkofer, Esper and Howlett (2016) examined consumer responses to the disclosure of limited inventory availability in an online business context; their research revealed an interesting finding that runs counter to the prediction that disclosure of limited inventory availability would reduce the dissatisfaction of stock-out situations.

Returns are three times more prevalent for online retailers, according to the National Retailer Federation (2015), and have been among the area of lowest satisfaction with shoppers over this five-year study; thus, the area of returns is one that most retailers should improve. In parallel, a recent survey of UPS (Ivory and Barker, 2016) underlines how the store returns provide an opportunity for retailers to save the sale or develop a loyal customer. A successful experience starts with order fulfilment that includes the necessary paperwork to complete the transaction. The in-store experience must include well-trained and helpful associates, short queues and accessible counters that facilitate convenient shopping. And, finally, the research shows 45% of the sample made an additional purchase when processing a return on a website.

Logistics operations where channel transition has led to several changes and improvements can be summarised as follows: inventory, picking, assortment, delivery, returns, organisation and the information technology (IT) system. Managing these changes implies a significant investment in infrastructure, knowledge and processes for warehousing and distribution. In the following paragraph, we will highlight the main implications for each step, reporting the key findings of a recent study about transition from the multichannel to omnichannel context (Chopra, 2016; Hübner, Wollenburg and Holzapfel, 2016; Kotzab Herbert, Hübner, Kuhn and Wollenburg, 2016).

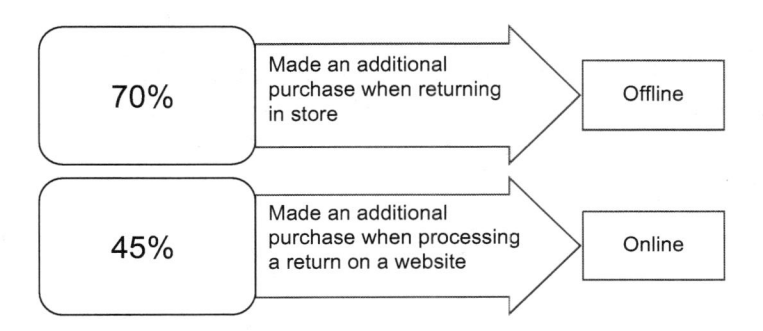

Figure 4.2 Offline versus online purchases
Adapted from Ivory and Barker (2016)

Inventory system

When operating in a multichannel environment, it is possible to decide among three main warehouse categories based on the degree of integration between inventory and picking processes:

(a) The first warehouse type is constituted by separated inventories or/and separated warehouses with separated inventory pickup for shipment for consumers (online orders) and store (offline orders).
(b) The second type has the same inventory for both offline and online channels but separate picking zones.
(c) The third type of warehouse has both inventory and picking unified for all channels. In addition, it is possible to use stores as inventory for web orders (see the Toys "R" Us case at the beginning of this chapter for an example).

Recent research reported that the transition from type (a) to type (c) is based on years of experience in managing different channels. So basically, companies that have recently joined the online channel are likely to maintain inventory and picking separated for the two channels. On the contrary, companies that are well established in both environments usually aim at unifying inventory and picking, unless they keep them separated for legal issues (for instance, online and offline channels are two separate legal entities). A full integration of inventory requires a certain level of multichannel process experience (Kull, Barratt, Sodero and Rabinovich, 2013; Bell, Gallino and Moreno, 2014; Hübner et al., 2016).

Picking processes

As stated for inventory, a common picking zone for online and offline channels would lead companies to improve their warehouse efficiency, using the same space and the same personnel for all channels. When unifying the picking process, two alternatives can be chosen. The first is to pick both online and offline orders at the same time. The second (less used) is to pick up in different time slots for each channel. Whatever the choice would be, the common goal of integrating picking across channels is to improve efficiency and lower the costs, particularly for online orders, where small amounts of products are picked compared with the offline orders (the store orders) (Hübner et al., 2015). For example, in today's omnichannel business environment, where accuracy and velocity are more important than ever a "pick to light" system can be implemented to enhance the capabilities and the productivity of the employees, particularly in high density warehouse.

Assortment

Omnichannel integration implies decisions on the breadth and depth of assortment for each channel. First, the number of stock keeping units (SKU) and the relative inventory level for each unit represent an important issue for companies. As shelf space is limited, retailers cannot offer limitless stock keeping units to the online environments, although virtual context serves to extend and offer a broader range of products compared with the offline context. Usually, those retailers that offer a small online assortment are those that have been present with a Web shop for less than three years (Hübner et al., 2016). Then, they gradually extend their online assortment until reaching the size of the offline assortment and then exceed it.

Delivery velocity

Shipping products implies of course some changes due to the integration of different channels. In addition, particularly for online channels, the delivery of products represents the touchpoints for final customers and plays a key role in determining customer value and loyalty. So, it needs a close attention from suppliers. Time in this case is one of the main elements of success and the competition on time is one the most challenging issue for companies to differentiate in the market. Nevertheless, the disadvantage of being fast is the cost of providing a short delivery time, which of course cannot be transferred to final customers.

To allow integration among channels there are several options of delivering and collecting products. One of the most used now is the *pick-up service*, which consists of allowing customers who purchased online to pick up goods at a store. Most of the time, this service is free. This service can be distinguished into click and collect (C&C) and reserve and collect (R&C).

C&C offers the opportunity to collect products already bought online in the offline store and the product is sent from a warehouse to the store. This service is increasingly being requested by customers as they purchase items online and then have the option to pick them up at a brick-and-mortar store. Most e-tailers aim at using it, although it is challenging to implement and become a seamless solution for both parties (Ternstrand et al., 2015). Product assortment plays a key role along with the decision about what strategy needs to be followed – that is, whether the customer should be allowed to choose from the total assortment or from a part of it to keep delivery costs low. The goal would be to have the total assortment also in the online channel to improve the customer experience and raise sales. Only in this case, this practice would be perceived as routine for consumers and stores. The reality is that today this service is sub-optimised and the customer must still queue at a regular checkout; she/he cannot see the product (often put in a brown box by warehouse staff). Consequently, we are quite far from providing a seamless solution (Ternstrand et al., 2015).

R&C is an option similar to C&C, which allows checkout to happen after the customer views the product in person. The customer reserves an item online and collects it and pays for it at a brick-and-mortar shop. This does not change the fundamentals of the supply chain, but requires brick-and-mortar retailers to efficiently organise the inventory using a powerful order management system. R&C connects the inventories in warehouses to inventories in stores. However, fewer retailers offer this service, while most of them adopt C&C (Hübner et al., 2016).

Another option is provided by *delivery lockers*, which are placed in convenient locations such as train stations and grocery stores. Consumers can open them using a code provided to the customer in connection with a purchase online. The same service can be used for returning the product. The negative aspect of lockers might be the lack of dynamism particularly in periods of highs sales.

Same-day delivery is another change in delivery velocity that requires companies to deliver the product the same day it has been purchased and might represent a source of competitive advantage. A recent survey reported that nearly 25% of consumers are willing to pay significant premiums for the privilege of same-day or instant delivery (Joerss et al., 2016). At the same time, it requires that the product ordered is in stock in a brick-and-mortar store or a warehouse that is located close to a major city and is delivered the same day to the customer. The change in consumers' expectations about speediness of delivery processes will strongly modify the transportation mode, particularly in the last mile. The adoption of autonomous ground vehicles with parcel lockers, drones and bike couriers would be the most used means of transport in the future (Joerss et al., 2016). Several companies are just in the early stages of a multiyear effort to adapt operations to meet those challenges, by increasing capacity and efficiency, including through expanded automation.

Drop-shipping is another way to create an efficient distribution of the product and allows customers to ship an order from a 3PL provider. This leads online retailers to diminish their inventory costs and warehouse space. Nevertheless, this practice cannot be adopted for all products, and it should depend on the industry. For instance, fashion products usually are ordered by customers of several brands and drop-shipping would require collecting multiple deliveries from the various manufacturers for delivery to the customer.

Product returns management

A customer's need, which is satisfied in an efficient and effective way through value-added selling, leads to repeat purchases and customer loyalty; managing returns seems to be an influencing factor for all the companies, as a supplier chain manager in the footwear industry reported to us:' . . . a customer, from a returns perspective, can be made loyal if he has a positive experience, otherwise he [sic] doesn't buy from you anymore'.

With the presence of different channels where customers can buy products, there are also multichannels where they can choose to return products. The returns mode represents the options that consumers have to return goods and also how suppliers manage product returns. The impact of managing returns has changed over the years, becoming an increasingly important aspect of the firm's business life to deal with. Managing the returns flow might play a strategic role through value creation and through the development of loyalty with the final customer. Firms must evaluate and know how to exploit the potential benefits of return flows and they must understand how to use them, for example to enter new markets. In the past, the relationship with the customer was not deeply considered because the attention of the firm was focused on the wrong sales forecast, on forward logistics and on production planning. Nowadays, the importance of the customer point of view is considered one of the driving factors and a huge amount of money is spent on marketing liberal returns policies. Loyalty is an important factor that is supported in making returns or credit decisions outside the 14-day period for Europe, for example.

The available options for customers are mainly two: shipping return products by postal shipments or in-store consignment. Not all companies allow customers to choose the returns mode; most of them in fact, separate the way to ship the return of products based on the channel. Hence, online products will be returned by postal shipment, while brick-and-mortar goods will be returned in-store. However, in an omnichannel context the option to return products across channels is becoming a must-have for companies. In addition, giving the opportunity to return products in-store that were bought online not only improves customer satisfaction but also provides retailers with the opportunity to cross-sell and upsell during a customer's store visit (Zhang et al., 2010). It is true, in fact, that customers expect lenient return policies, particularly for the online channel. This is meant in terms of a long and free period to return the products and the opportunity to ship the product where preferred. Therefore, this service has become one of the key elements for being competitive in the market and a key determinant in the customer's decision-making process. From a logistics perspective, however, this practice is associated with an increase in costs of transportation, handling and managing of returns products. This represents an additional flow for companies to manage, and the main challenge will be to optimise returns costs.

One way to reduce costs can be reached, for instance, by diminishing the return rate derived from a lack of information or product images online. Another attempt to provide cost savings is to improve the control of product quality and reduce the delivery of defective products. The way retailers decide to take delivery of the returns product – directly to a returns centre or keeping things in-store – may depend on several aspects: type of product, sector and company size. The costs of warehouses for returns depends on company organisation and efficiency. Often, returns are kept in a separate flow with a specific allocation in the warehouse. These areas are in general less efficient and provide less control over inventory. Therefore, there is room to improve returns efficiency and cost minimisation. Focusing on customer service is one way to develop customer loyalty and to ensure a stable long-period demand. For example, Zappos has been one of the first online sellers to offer a lenient and generous returns policy and free shipping. The return policy the company adopted tempted customers to buy many items, to try them at home and to send back everything they did not like, without providing justifications. The retention mantra has been outstanding customer service. According to CEO

Craig Adkins, 'Our best customers have the highest returns rates, but they are also the ones that spend the most money with us and are our most profitable customers'. His company's free shipping and returns policy is a perfect way for hesitant shoppers to mitigate the risks of online purchases – and it is also a smart retention tactic.

Organisation

Organising and managing different channels constitutes a challenge for companies, particularly for those of small and medium sizes. A recent study reported that 39% of companies operate online and offline channels separately, although 84% agreed with the statement that they were dissatisfied with this separation of organisational units (Hübner et al., 2016). This is because both channels could be operated in a more efficient way if logistics were to be managed and handled by the same organisation. To support their evolving customer and sales model, B2B companies need to decide what and how to reconfigure in terms of financial and human resources across sales channels. This means identifying which skills need to be reallocated, what data and analytics resources are needed, what processes need to be reorganised and which resources are needed.

Information technology systems

To simplify and provide more visibility among channels, IT systems play a great role in overcoming the complexity of managing multiple channels. IT systems help companies to update real-time information and manage the huge amount of data about orders, inventory and deliveries for each channel, allowing companies to receive channel-integrated information and to provide customers with the most updated information about product availability and tracking of their orders. This has huge impact for the entire supply chain, where IT infrastructure integration is needed to improve information across firms, turning fragmented, functional and silo-oriented supply chain processes into integrated, cross-functional and inter-firm supply chain processes (Rai, Patnayakuni and Seth, 2006).

In particular, the digitalisation of supply chains has forced the need for an inventory visibility that eliminates any barriers and attempts to integrate all channels. This requires a robust order management system (OMS). This allows integration among order and deliveries, providing companies with all information regarding inventory, delivery options and customer information. An OMS shares real-time information about the whole order cycle, from the order to the final delivery, coming from all channels. Information is collected regardless of the channel it comes from, providing an overall picture of the inventory status; it provides information about store, in-transit inventory, internal delivery centres and drop-ship vendors, as well as releasing updated data about store fulfilment and order details. This allows more efficient and more effective operating that improves customer service (sharing with the customer real-time information about assortment availability, order status and tracking of goods). Thanks to digitalisation, warehouse management can benefit from the so-called 'Internet of Things', which enhances the coordination among products, machines and employees. This leads to a better integration and to productivity improvement. Considering the product, RFID systems, which can be labelled as 'Tagging Technologies, have allowed better product tracking, improved visibility and better accuracy of fulfilment processes. In addition, the Internet of Things has provided warehouses with machines and vehicles that follow optimal journeys with a better communication across 'machine to machine' and 'machine to human'. From a workforce perspective, the Internet of Things is improving connections among employees through several technologies; one of them is the 'wearable device', which helps workforces to improve their communication and interaction among other employees. This helps in determining not only employees' level of productivity but also their level of stress and health. It also tracks the journey she or he follows within the warehouse.

To summarise, these changes derived from digitalisation and omnichannel phenomena imply a redefinition of supply chain activities with all B2B players involved. In addition, a rethink of strategies from a marketing perspective is required. Starting from the belief that supply chain members can no longer think of their online and offline channels separately, it is also important to understand how to succeed in an omnichannel context, providing customers with a satisfying experience.

First, be consumer-centric: understand not only customers' characteristics but also which path they follow to purchase across channels. This allows companies to provide customers with ad hoc offers and personalised information. This means building a sort of 'personal supply chain', which implies the structuring of a holistic shopping experience for the customer instead of different offerings from separate channels. It requires all employees of a company to be aware of this goal, with specific training and sharing of information to achieve a successful omnichannel experience. The result will enable supply chains to react to any disruptions from upstream to downstream, and even anticipate them, by fully modelling the network, the nodes and the link, creating scenarios and adjusting the supply chain in real time as conditions change.

Second, do not treat all countries as a unique market, as going digital means dealing with different regulatory requirements, technology differences and cultural specificity. So, different strategies and market adaptation are highly recommended.

Consequently, yet importantly, going digital does not require us to underestimate and sub-manage the brick-and-mortar business. Stores should keep their role and importance and retailers should rethink and improve the in-store experience, maintaining a high level of customer service and providing skilled employees and services. A firm's goal should be to have as much information as possible about all aspects of its supply chain and its customers; for instance information about stock visibility, data quality and level of optimisation of transport, data about planning integration level and delivery accuracy, etc. To achieve these goals, companies need to master micro-segmentation, splitting the supply chain into several micro chain segments, each of them based on customers' requirements and the company's own capabilities.

Finally, digital technologies have greatly affected the capabilities and strategies of suppliers, manufacturers and retailers. They have required firms to develop new business models, new operational capabilities and perspectives, inside and outside the company, to revamp their supply chains to be more competitive and transparent in the new business context. This absolutely helps an understanding of the customers in order to find different recipes to keep customers loyal.

References

Bell, D. R., Gallino, S. and Moreno, A. (2014) 'How to win in an omnichannel world', *MIT Sloan Management Review*, 56(1), 45.

Chopra, S. (2016) 'How omni-channel can be the future of retailing', *Decision*, 43(2), 135–144.

Falk, T., Schepers, J., Hammerschmidt, M. and Bauer, H. (2007) 'Identifying cross-channel dissynergies for multichannel service providers', *Journal of Service Research*, 10(2), 143–160.

Goldsby, T. J. and Zinn, W. (2016) 'Technology innovation and new business models: can logistics and supply chain research accelerate the evolution?', *Journal of Business Logistics*, 37(2), 80–81.

Herhausen, D., Binder, J., Schoegel, M. and Herrmann, A. (2015) 'Integrating bricks with clicks: retailer-level and channel-level outcomes of online – offline channel integration', *Journal of Retailing*, 91(2), 309–325.

Hübner, A., Holzapfel, A. and Kuhn, H. (2015) 'Operations management in multi-channel retailing: an exploratory study', *Operations Management Research*, 8(3–4), 84–100.

Hübner, A., Wollenburg, J. and Holzapfel, A. (2016) 'Retail logistics in the transition from multi-channel to omni-channel', *International Journal of Physical Distribution & Logistics Management*, 46(6/7), 562–583.

Hübner, A., Kuhn, H., and Wollenburg, J. (2016) 'Last mile fulfilment and distribution in omni-channel grocery retailing: A strategic planning framework', *International Journal of Retail & Distribution Management*, 44(3), 228–247.

Ivory, A. and Barker, S. (2016) UPS pulse of the online shoppers, UPS White Paper, June 2016. Available at https://pressroom.ups.com/pressroom/ContentDetailsViewer.page?ConceptType=FactSheets&id=1465325363052-863. Accessed 28th December 2016.

Joerss, M. Florian Neuhaus, F.and Jürgen Schröder, J. (2016) 'How customer demands are reshaping last-mile delivery.' Available at http://www.mckinsey.com/industries/travel-transport-and-logistics/our-insights/how-customer-demands-are-reshaping-last-mile-delivery accessed December 2016.

Kull, T. J., Barratt, M., Sodero, A. C. and Rabinovich, E. (2013) 'Investigating the effects of daily inventory record inaccuracy in multichannel retailing', *Journal of Business Logistics*, 34(3), 189–208.

National Retail Federation. (2015) *Consumer returns in the retail industry*. Available at https://nrf.com/sites/default/files/Images/Media%20Center/NRF%20Retail%20Return%20Fraud%20Final_0.pdf. Accessed on 20 December 2016.

Peinkofer, S. T., Esper, T. L. and Howlett, E. (2016) 'Hurry! Sale ends soon: the impact of limited inventory availability disclosure on consumer responses to online stockouts', *Journal of Business Logistics*, 37(3), 231–246.

Rai, A., Patnayakuni, R. and Seth, N. (2006) 'Firm performance impacts of digitally enabled supply chain integration capabilities', *MIS Quarterly*, 30(2), 225–246.

Ternstrand, C., Selldin, E., Virta, N. and Linder, S. (2015) *Omni-channel retail: a Deloitte point of view*. Available at httpshttps://www2.deloitte.com/content/dam/Deloitte/se/Documents/technology/Omni-channel-2015.pdf. Accessed on 20th January 2017.

Zhang, J., Farris, P., Irvin, J., Kushwaha, T., Steen-burghe, T. and Weitz, B (2010) 'Crafting integrated multichannel retailing strategies', *Journal of Interactive Marketing*, 24(2), 168–180.

Ziobro, P. (2016) 'As Web sales spike, retailers scramble to ship from stores', *Wall Street Journal*. Available at www.wsj.com/articles/retailers-revamp-strategy-to-handle-holiday-season-demand-1480588202?mod=djemlogistics. Accessed on 9th December 2016.

5 Theory, methods and practice for measuring customer loyalty

Introduction

This chapter begins by identifying different methodologies that could be suitable for approaching and measuring customer loyalty, with a particular focus on the B2B context. To achieve this, the chapter opens with an overview of complexity theory and then it will apply a multi-step approach of analysis to two cases.

Although the extant literature helps identify various predictors of customer loyalty, past studies have concentrated exclusively on the 'net effects' of these antecedents. Yet, there are theoretical reasons to suggest that these effects may be more complicated than they first appear. According to complexity theory, in the real world, 'relationships between variables can be non-linear, with abrupt switches occurring; thus, the same "cause" can, in specific circumstances, produce different effects' (Urry, 2005, p. 4). In line with this theorising, we will attempt to show how firms participating in B2B markets can achieve high levels of customer loyalty under different configurations of several variables (for instance, perceived offer quality, service support, and personal interaction). To address this goal, we employ qualitative comparative analysis (QCA). This method uses Boolean algebra rules to identify which of the attribute combinations, if any, act as sufficient or necessary conditions for the outcome. The QCA method assumes that the influence of attributes on a specific outcome (in this case, customer loyalty in a B2B context) depends on how the attributes are combined.

To summarise, beyond more 'standards approaches' such as statistics and quantitative methods (e.g., structural equation modelling, multiple regression analysis, analysis of variance [ANOVA]), this chapter will provide a qualitative approach that will explain the complex world of understanding and measuring customer loyalty.

Applying complexity theory to customer loyalty in a supply chain context

Typically, there is a significant asymmetry of knowledge between the supplier and the customer, along with knowledge transfer difficulties and the complexity of evaluating the quality of the offering. A positive evaluation of this should contribute to maintaining business relationships and preventing switches to other suppliers. The increasing complexity of understanding the roles, relationships and drivers among buyers, suppliers, manufacturers and other parties in the B2B context is part of the challenge to understanding and maintaining loyalty. To deliver better value throughout the supply chain to the end consumer, it is important to understand these players' role in value propositions and the relative complexity between the supplier/manufacturer and the customer. Modern customers are more likely than those of the past to switch suppliers, but the literature and the practice itself led us to believe this behaviour can be attenuated by different combinations of attributes or resources, leading to differential loyalty gains for companies with more effective processes for dealing with flows. Complexities can arise when the buyer-supplier relationship involves a plethora of exchanged goods and services with varying levels of switching costs and customer satisfaction. Gummesson (2008) underlined how marketing is complex as there are several variables interacting. As in a business context unique situations are potentially without limit, network theory, which is part of the complexity theory, can be suitable to face and manage such uniqueness and complexity. For example, 'strategy' can refer to a set of guidelines that influence decisions and behaviour, and the complexity of strategic interactions, whether in chess, soccer, politics or in business, makes it essential to adopt simplifying strategies to guide decisions (Levy, 1994). The complexity of interactions and relationships along the supply chain is such that one cannot easily predict in terms of outcome how the system will operate under various antecedents. Indeed, Simon (1962) defined a complex system as being composed of interconnected subsystems that work together with a specific form of hierarchy. Several theories and a body of research have tried to interpret the complex system – from cybernetics to general systems theory, through catastrophe theory and chaos theory, to name a few (Levy, 1994; Simon, 1996; Anderson, 1999; Mele and Polese, 2011; Byrne and Callaghan, 2013; Wu, Yeh, Huan and Woodside, 2014). In organisation science, there are different levels of complexity: vertical, as the number of organisational hierarchies; horizontal, as the number of departments and job titles across the organisation; or spatial, as the number of geographical locations (Anderson, 1999).

An organisation must try to match the complexity of an organisation's structure with the complexity of the macro- and microenvironments. Because of the complex reality in which the phenomenon of interest manifests itself, complexity theory tenets can help provide a more accurate understanding of what generates a phenomenon. Table 5.1 summarises the core tenets of complexity theory.

Consistent with complexity theory and its tenets, this chapter investigates how firms can achieve high levels of customer loyalty under different configurations of antecedents. Research on complexity theory indicates that if a system passes a particular threshold with minor changes in the controlling variables, switches occur such that a liquid turns into gas, or a large number of apathetic people suddenly tip into a forceful movement for change (Gladwell, 2006), that 'such tipping points give rise to unexpected structures and events' (Urry, 2005, p. 5). This highlights the complexity of the relationship between an antecedent and an outcome variable, and the possibility that the relationship would change

Table 5.1 Tenets of complexity theory

Tenets	
T1	A simple antecedent condition may be necessary, but a simple antecedent condition is rarely sufficient for predicting a high or low score in an outcome condition.
T2	A complex antecedent condition of two or more simple conditions is sufficient for a consistently high score in an outcome condition – the recipe principle.
T3	A model that is sufficient is not necessary for an outcome having a high score to occur – the equifinality principle.
T4	Recipes indicating a second outcome (e.g., rejection) are unique and not the mirror opposites of recipes of a different outcome (e.g., acceptance) – the causal asymmetry principle.
T5	An individual feature (attribute or action) in a recipe can contribute positively or negatively to a specific outcome depending on the presence or absence of the other ingredients in the recipes.
T6	For high Y scores, a given recipe is relevant for some but not all cases; coverage is less than 1.00 for any one recipe. A few exceptions occur for high X scores for a given recipe that works well for predicting high Y scores.

Source: Woodside (2014)

based on different configurations. Definitions of complexity commonly used in the organisational domain are often tied to the concept of a system.

This perspective is supported by network theory, which forms a part of complexity theory. Network theory indicates that a network is made up of nodes (e.g., individuals, firms) and relationships and interaction among the nodes. Infusing all disciplines for its cross-cutting content, complexity reflects the attention that scholars of different disciplines give to this issue (Barile and Polese, 2010). Applying complexity theory allows scholars to have a deeper and richer perspective of data, and a superior predictive accuracy of using algorithms versus regression models, particularly in the social sciences (Gigerenzer, 1991; Sterman and Wittenberg, 1999; Gigerenzer and Brighton, 2009; Woodside, 2015). However, it is challenging for a practitioner to convert the complexity of his or her real business world by selecting a number from a scale. Nevertheless, social science complexity analyses reveal how there is order and disorder within various systems. In other words, complexity theory requires different types of marketing reactions or supply chain responsiveness when a business context increases in complexity and turbulence. As the environment context, processes, product, suppliers and customers become more complex, the company must focus its scarce resources on those activities that will give the best result. This is one of the reasons for the emergence of constructs such as supply chain agility, supply chain resiliency and customer value anticipation, to name a few. The degree of complexity is derived from the structural properties of the system as determined by the number and variety of elements defining the supply chain and their interactions (e.g., the number of participants, facilities and warehouses, products, transportation links, information and financial flows) (Choi and Krause, 2006; Manuj and Sahin, 2011).

Crafting and testing theories of main and interaction effects fails to capture the complexity inherent in the B2B context. Complexity theory helps to devise hypotheses that are less overly simplistic and that offer better and different findings – above all, that offer a potential contribution to theory. Understanding the drivers is critical when devising strategies to manage the resulting complexity. It would be more useful to transcend to a complexity theory perspective on B2B inter-firm relationships and outcomes, particularly in research such as ours where we included a study of dynamic relationships with independent variables (or complex antecedent conditions) affecting dependent variables (or outcome conditions) in different time periods.

Complexity theory suggests that numerous variables interact without the constraints of limited unique situations, that change is ordinary and that processes are not linear but iterative (Woodside and Baxter, 2013; Woodside, 2014; Wu et al., 2014). In summary, complexity theory helps provide a more accurate and comprehensive picture of customer behaviour by accounting for the dynamic and complex relationships among the variables under investigation (Russo, Confente, Gligor and Autry, 2016). As such, in our exemplar cases, instead of analysing the main effects of certain predictors, we seek to determine configurations (i.e., combinations of antecedents) that help explain customer loyalty in the B2B context.

In the following paragraphs, we will introduce and describe two approaches of data analysis for the same B2B scenario. First, we will contextualise the case, industry and sample that we adopted in previous studies for different purposes (Russo et al., 2016; Russo et al., 2017); after that we will define the variables of interest in our model. Such variables will be analysed following a more traditional approach (multiple regression analysis) and then through QCA using fuzzy sets.

In the second part of the chapter, a second case related to LSQ will be analysed adopting the same multi-step approach.

Study A. Measuring value perception and loyalty in the business-to-business context

Data collection, survey development and sampling

The aim of Study A was to explore the perception of value drivers in a B2B health care service context and their impact on customer loyalty. The focus is on the repeated purchase intent dimension of customer loyalty. Repurchase intent has been described as customers' anticipation of purchasing again, their commitment to retain the relationship or intent to continue a relationship with a provider for the foreseeable future.

The health care industry was selected for several reasons. Investigating the health care industry through tools commonly applied in business management research has a wide diffusion (Berry and Bendapudi, 2007; Crié and Chebat, 2013), with the complexity of the product offering driving final customers to search for advice from trustworthy and reliable sources. As such, this industry represents a good example of a changing marketing channel structure that has emerging actors who have adopted a larger role in the manufacturer–end consumer exchange.

The unit of analysis was business customers operating within this industry and how they perceive drivers in their supplier's value delivery. During the initial stages of the research, we used qualitative inquiry to develop the relevant constructs from the customers' perspectives. Specifically, we conducted one-to-two-hour semi-structured interviews with 23 audiologists operating small businesses in the Italian hearing aid distribution industry. The goal of this step was to understand in depth the characteristics of this industry, its marketing channels (market competition, consumer change) and the different customer value drivers, as well as to understand better how the supplier relationships have changed over time in response to ever-demanding customer orientations. Audiologists – our unit of analysis – are health care professionals and can provide and set up hearing aids; at the same time, they are small entrepreneurs, running small private businesses and thus were ideal participants for our study in the B2B context.

Such professionals purchase products or services from the hearing aid suppliers and are enabled by law to resell them to hearing-impaired end users. They represent a facilitator for the final customer because they evaluate and determine the best value offering for her or him, providing advice and assistance to the final customers or patients. As such, audiologists serve as a primary commercial distribution channel for hearing aid manufacturers.

We defined a list of participant criteria to determine the inclusion or exclusion of participants to our final sample. Respondents were selected among those health care professionals who:

a)   were enabled by law to resell hearing aids,
b)   were currently operating a business at the retail level, and
c)   had freedom of supplier selection.

We selected 500 health care professionals who met the criteria and sent them an email with a link to a secure Web survey. This survey was completed after a pretest that refined the structure of the survey and the items involved in the survey.

A pilot survey was administered as a pre-test among 20 participants. Following refinement, the survey was distributed to the remaining qualified participants. We obtained a 64.4% response rate.

Measurement of variables

Based on the findings of the pilot studies, the finalised survey was administered. Questions were divided into two main sections. Section A evaluated the demographic characteristics of respondents and the characteristics of the audiologist–key supplier relationship (e.g., experience with hearing aid products expressed in terms of years, length of the partnership with the main supplier expressed in terms of years, total expenditure with their main supplier expressed in terms of percentage of expenditure over the total expenditure). Section B contained seven-point Likert scales devised to tap customer loyalty (our dependent variable), the perception of customer value, customer satisfaction, perceived offer quality, product specification, personal interaction, service support, product returns management and perceived switching costs for the audiologists in the sample frame.

All measures were adapted from existing scales. In particular, customer loyalty was assessed using three scale items proposed by Blocker, Flint, Myers and Slater (2011). Customer value was measured using three scale items from Blocker (2011) and Ulaga and Eggert (2006). Customer satisfaction was evaluated using three scale items adapted from Lam, Shankar, Erramilli and Murthy (2004) and Flint, Blocker and Boutin (2011). Offer quality, product specification, personal interaction and service support items were measured using three scale items for each construct taken from Ulaga and Eggert (2006) and Blocker (2011). Product returns management was assessed using three scale items adapted from Mollenkopf, Rabinovich, Laseter and Boyer (2007). Perceived switching costs was measured using five scale items evaluating aspects such as time, money, effort and risk associated with change of supplier technology (Lam et al., 2004).

To analyse our data set, we propose two approaches, one based on statistical analysis and another one based on QCA. Both are used to answer to the same question: what dimensions lead to high customer loyalty?

Method 1. Multiple regression analysis

Regression analysis has been used in the social sciences since Galton introduced it in the 1870s (Armstrong, 2011). This method of data analysis aims at estimating the existence of the influence (or its absence) of each hypothesised predictor (independent variables; i.e., in our case, offer quality) on an outcome variable (the dependent variable; i.e., in our case, customer loyalty). Such an effect is considered by isolating the influence of other independent variables in an equation that encompasses several variables (two or more dimensions). This analysis approach usually compares different models that include or exclude certain variables in order to explain how such independent variables have significant or not significant 'net effects' combined with the presence or absence of other independent variables.

Such relationships tested through Multiple Regression Analysis (MRA) as well as through SEM (Structural Equation Modelling) analysis can be considered as symmetrical, where low values of X lead to low values of Y, while high values of X are associated with high values of Y. When X and Y are highly correlated (for instance when r is greater than 0.60), the same data set includes cases of high X and low Y, and cases of low X and high Y; however, contrarian cases are ignored in most studies (Woodside, 2014).

Figure 5.1 shows this relationship and, as can been observed, all the cases (named a, b, c, etc.) lie on a straight line. One benefit from using regression analysis is that 'regression estimates become more conservative as uncertainty increases' (Armstrong, 2011, p. 4). In addition, control variables can be added to the model to account for potential differences in the outcome variable.

Overall, regression analysis can represent a good analysis for decision-making because it provides objectives and a systematic way to analyse data, although some problems might occur. The same can be said of SEM, which this chapter does not consider.

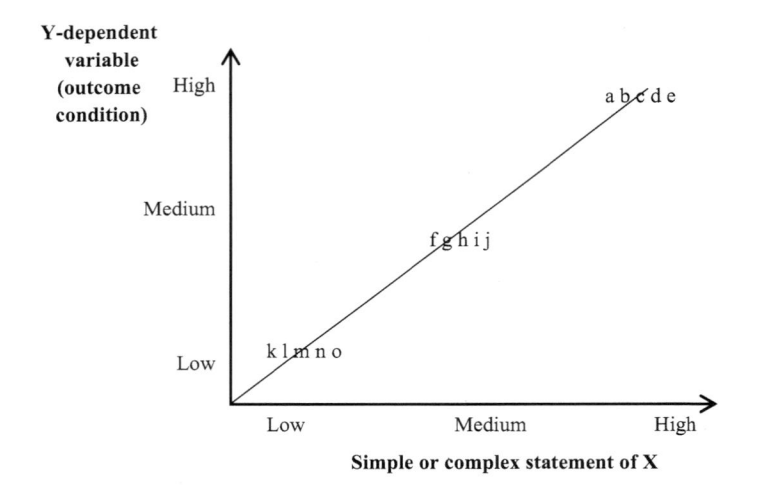

Figure 5.1 Symmetrical relationships between X and Y
Source: Our elaboration adapted from Woodside (2014)

Table 5.2 Descriptive statistics

Variables	Items	Min	Max	Mean	St. dev.
Offer quality (OQ)	3	1.333	7.000	5.035	1.092
Personal interaction (PI)	3	2.333	7.000	5.634	1.003
Service support (SS)	3	1.000	7.000	3.358	2.21
Product specification (PS)	3	1.000	7.000	4.397	1.761
Switching costs (SWI)	3	2.000	7.000	4.956	1.727
Product returns management (RET)	3	1.000	7.000	1.977	.950
Customer value (CV)	3	2.000	7.000	5.213	.744
Customer satisfaction (SAT)	3	2.000	7.000	5.365	.832
Customer loyalty (LOY)	3	2.670	7.000	5.585	.625

Analysis and results

Table 5.2 presents the minimum, maximum, means and standard deviations of the selected variables of Study A. On average, personal interaction represents the variable that respondents evaluated as being the most valuable (mean = 5.634), followed by offer quality (mean = 5.035). Among those dimensions that were evaluated by customers as low, product returns management is the lowest ranked (mean = 1.977), demonstrating a lack on the part of the supplier to solve problems related to product returns management. Interestingly, respondents were quite satisfied (mean = 5.365) and loyal (mean = 5.585).

Table 5.3 shows the correlations among variables. The results show that the correlations between the proposed independent variables were less than .70, indicating that multicollinearity is absent.

Table 5.3 Constructs correlation

	1	2	3	4	5	6	7	8	9
1. Offer quality	1	.166(**)	−.487(**)	.726(**)	−.082	.164(**)	.411(**)	.529(**)	.396(**)
2. Personal interaction	−.166(**)	1	.484(**)	−.272(**)	.615(**)	.179(**)	.226(**)	.154(**)	.144(**)
3. Service support	−.487(**)	.484(**)	1	−.688(**)	.414(**)	.115(*)	.055	−.027	−.035
4. Product specification	.726(**)	−.272(**)	−.688(**)	1	−.015	.158(**)	.215(**)	.492(**)	.394(**)
5. Switching costs	−0.081	0.614	0.414★	−.015	1	.094(*)	.231(**)	.248(**)	.284(**)
6. Product returns	.164(**)	.179(**)	.115(*)	.158(**)	.094(*)	1	.048	.160(*)	.127(**)
7. Customer value	.411(**)	.226(**)	.055	.215(**)	.231(**)	.048	1	.448(**)	.328(**)
8. Customer satisfaction	.529(**)	.154(**)	−.027	.492(**)	.248(**)	.160(**)	.448(**)	1	.599(**)
9. Customer loyalty	.396(**)	.144(**)	−.035	.394(**)	.284(**)	.127(*)	.328(**)	599(**)	1

★ Correlation is significant at the 0.05 level (1-tailed).
★★ Correlation is significant at the 0.01 level (1-tailed).

Given the assurance of validity based on the initial analyses, regression analysis was then used to test the hypotheses using SPSS software (see Table 5.4). Hence, we estimated the following equation:

$$\begin{aligned}
Customer\,loyalty = {} & \beta_0 + \beta_1 OQ + \beta_2 PI + \beta_3 SS + \beta_4 PS + \beta_5 SWI \\
& + \beta_6 RET + \beta_7 CV + \beta_8 SAT + \beta_9 GENDER\,\beta_{10}\,AGE \\
& + \beta_{11} EXPERIENCE + \beta_{12} PARTNER \\
& + \beta_{13} EXPENDITURE + \varepsilon_i
\end{aligned} \tag{1}$$

In this equation, customer loyalty represents our dependent variable, while the other variables are our independent variables. We also added some control variables, such as year of experience in the industry (EXPERIENCE), length of partnership (PARTNERSHIP) and percentage of expenditure with the main supplier (EXPENDITURE), plus some demographic characteristics such as gender and age. The explanatory power of our model (R^2 457) was high. Table 5.4 represents the main results and the significant and not significant relationships of the independent variables with loyalty.

Considering the relationship among the independent variables and the dependent variable, in our case customer loyalty, we found that few variables have a positive and significant relationship. These are offer quality, perceived switching

Table 5.4 Regression analysis for customer loyalty

	Estimate	Std. Error	t value	$Pr(>|t|)$
(Constant)	−1.098	11.075	−.099	.921
Offer quality	.149	.041	2.054	.041*
Personal interaction	.047	.040	.731	.465
Service support	−.012	.024	−.137	.891
Product specification	−.025	.036	.245	.806
Switching costs	.148	.023	2.371	.018*
Product returns	−.005	.032	−.104	.917
Customer value	.041	.045	.763	.446
Customer satisfaction	.457	.047	7.348	.000***
Gender	.021	.057	.459	.646
Age	.183	.006	2.627	.009*
Experience	−.272	.052	−4.257	.000***
Partnership	−.080	.050	−1.595	.112
Expenditure	.074	.020	1.621	.106

Signif. codes: 0 '***' 0.001 '**' 0.01 '*' 0.05 '.' 0.1 ' ' 1
Residual standard error: 0.67 on 302 degrees of freedom
Multiple R-squared: 0.676, Adjusted R-squared: 0.432

costs and customer satisfaction. Thus, high values of perceived offer quality ($\beta = .149$, p value $< .05$) and customer satisfaction ($\beta = .457$, p value $< .001$) lead to high levels of customer loyalty.

The same is true for perceived switching costs: when they were perceived as very high, customers were loyal ($\beta = .148$, p value $< .05$). At this time, we do not know whether in this latter case, customers were also satisfied with the supplier's offering or whether they stuck with her or him only because of such high costs. Among the demographics, gender was not significant in its impact on loyalty, while it appears that older customers were more loyal than younger customers ($\beta = .183$, p value $< .05$). Considering the effect of the control variables, it seems that the length of partnership or the amount of expenditure caused by the main supplier did not affect customer loyalty, while the experience in the industry had a negative and significant effect on loyalty ($\beta = -.272$, p value $< .001$).

Method 2. Qualitative comparative analysis using fuzzy set qualitative comparative analysis software

To address the need to understand better a phenomenon and its relationship with other dimensions within a complex scenario, recent research has attempted to adopt and apply other methods to analyse data and information. In particular, the use of statistical analysis to represent reality might be not suitable in certain cases. Such symmetric tests, in fact, rarely match well with reality, except when testing the association of two or more items to measure the same construct (coefficient alpha is a symmetric test, for instance). Conversely, asymmetric tests reflect realities well given that the causes of high Y scores usually differ substantially from the causes of low Y scores (i.e., the principle of causal asymmetry, see Fiss, 2011).

It has been argued that the nearly rote statements of main effects and rote applications of MRA appearing in most academic studies in management-related sub-disciplines ignore the complexities inherent in realities and apparent in the data sets. With this in mind, Woodside and Baxter (2013) compared and contrasted the use of symmetric (e.g., MRA and SEM) versus asymmetric (e.g., analysis by quintiles and by fuzzy set QCA). The authors argued that symmetric tests consider accuracy in high values of X (an antecedent condition) indicating high values of Y (an outcome condition), and in low values of X indicating low values of Y. As argued, the focus on the net effects can be misleading for several reasons: the presence of counter cases to the observed net effects very often occur, and not all the cases in the data support a positive or negative relationship between X and Y. In addition, realities can include more than one combination to explain a phenomenon (outcome variable). The outcome depends on how the Xs are combined rather than on the levels of individual attributes per se (Ordanini, Parasuraman and Rubera, 2014). In contrast, asymmetric tests consider the accuracy of high values of X indicating high values of Y without predicting how low values of X relate to values of Y (Figure 5.2).

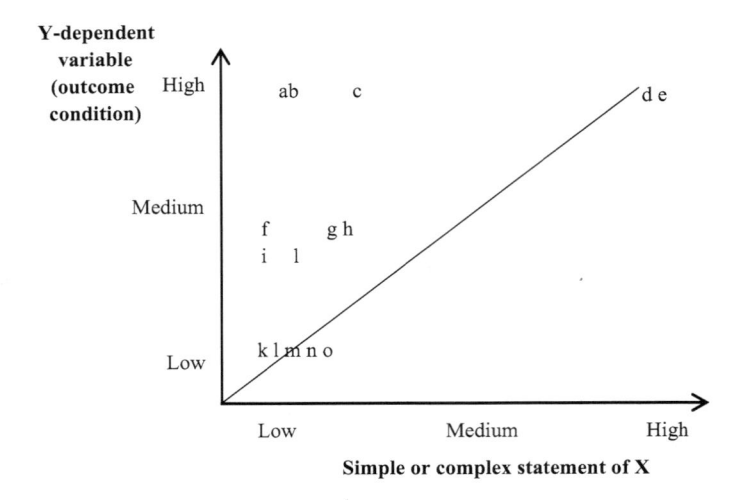

Figure 5.2 Asymmetrical relationships between X and Y

Source: Our elaboration adapted from Woodside (2014)

In the following paragraphs, we develop an alternative approach of data analysis that relies on the existence of asymmetric relationships among variables. In doing so, we adopt a multi-step data analysis, starting from the contrarian case analysis.

Implementation of contrarian analysis

Contrarian case analysis facilitates a better understanding of the complexity of a phenomenon and it confirms that substantial numbers of cases that display relationships that are counter to a negative (or positive) main effect between X and Y occur, even when the effect size of the reported X-Y relationship is large. For example, when X associates positively with Y with high correlation, it may occur that the same data set includes cases of high X and low Y and cases of low X and high Y. Most of the time, scholars ignore these contrarian cases in most reports (Woodside, 2014). A good starting point is represented by a quintile analysis, which includes dividing the respondent cases from the lowest to highest quintile for each measured construct and examining the relationships among two or more constructs (McClelland, 1998). Hsiao, Jaw, Huan and Woodside (2015) provide an outstanding example of such analysis, demonstrating such asymmetry through QCA for all four sets of relationships. Even when an effect size is large between two variables, cases exist in almost all large data sets that run counter to the main effects relationship. Our recent manuscript related to the customer loyalty context provides another useful example (Russo et al., 2016). We found the existence of contrarian cases in a scenario where the overall picture had confirmed the main large effect for constructs such as customer value, customer satisfaction and perceived switching costs. On the contrary, this did not happen for the product returns management construct, which had several negative contrarian cases in its relationship with loyalty. To demonstrate this, as can be seen in Figure 5.3, we developed a contingency table considering quintiles. We created such computation using SPSS software. Results confirm that product returns management is 'responsible for the changing/counter results'. Loyalty has a 'symmetric' relationship with customer value, satisfaction and perceived switching costs but asymmetric one for several cases in its relationship with product returns management (see the 'Negative contrarian cases' box in Figure 5.3). Regarding recovery responsiveness, we also have the case of positive contrarian analysis (see the box 'positive contrarian cases' box in Figure 5.3). When product returns receive high evaluation by respondents, this condition is not sufficient to create high loyalty as repurchase intent.

To provide further examples helping researchers to adopt contrarian analysis to demonstrate the relationship among variables, we conducted such analysis for all the variables related to Study A of the present chapter, and a selection of some relationships are demonstrated here. In Method 1 (MRA), some variables were significant and positively linked to customer loyalty, while others were not

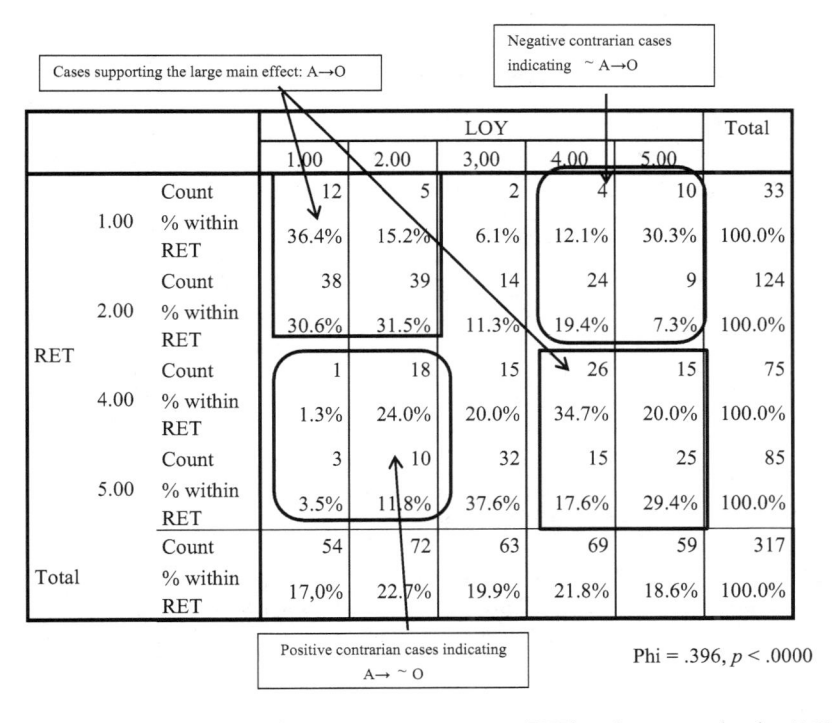

			LOY					Total
			1.00	2.00	3,00	4.00	5.00	
RET	1.00	Count	12	5	2	4	10	33
		% within RET	36.4%	15.2%	6.1%	12.1%	30.3%	100.0%
	2.00	Count	38	39	14	24	9	124
		% within RET	30.6%	31.5%	11.3%	19.4%	7.3%	100.0%
	4.00	Count	1	18	15	26	15	75
		% within RET	1.3%	24.0%	20.0%	34.7%	20.0%	100.0%
	5.00	Count	3	10	32	15	25	85
		% within RET	3.5%	11.8%	37.6%	17.6%	29.4%	100.0%
Total		Count	54	72	63	69	59	317
		% within RET	17,0%	22.7%	19.9%	21.8%	18.6%	100.0%

Cases supporting the large main effect: A→O

Negative contrarian cases indicating ~ A→O

Positive contrarian cases indicating A→ ~ O

Phi = .396, $p < .0000$

Figure 5.3 Two outcomes: product returns management (RET) and customer loyalty (LOY)

Note: A = antecedent condition; O = outcome condition

significant and not linked to the same outcome. We describe here an example of contrarian analysis of a significant relationship, that is, offer quality with customer loyalty, and another example of an insignificant relationship, that is, the case of service support with customer loyalty, to shed more light on the absence of such a link or on the presence of some contrarian cases that diminishes such a relationship.

Figure 5.4 shows the quintiles of offer quality and customer loyalty. Results confirm loyalty has a 'symmetric' relationship with offer quality, except for few contrarian cases that do not impact on the overall large main effect. Thus, when offer quality received a high evaluation by respondents, this attribute was sufficient to create high loyalty; also, when respondents were not satisfied with the quality of the offer, they were likely not to be loyal to the company.

Moving on from what regression analysis defined as not significant, an example of how contrarian analysis provides a deeper explanation of such results is provided in Figure 5.6. The antecedent variable taken as an example is the construct of service support (SS), which apparently did not have significant links

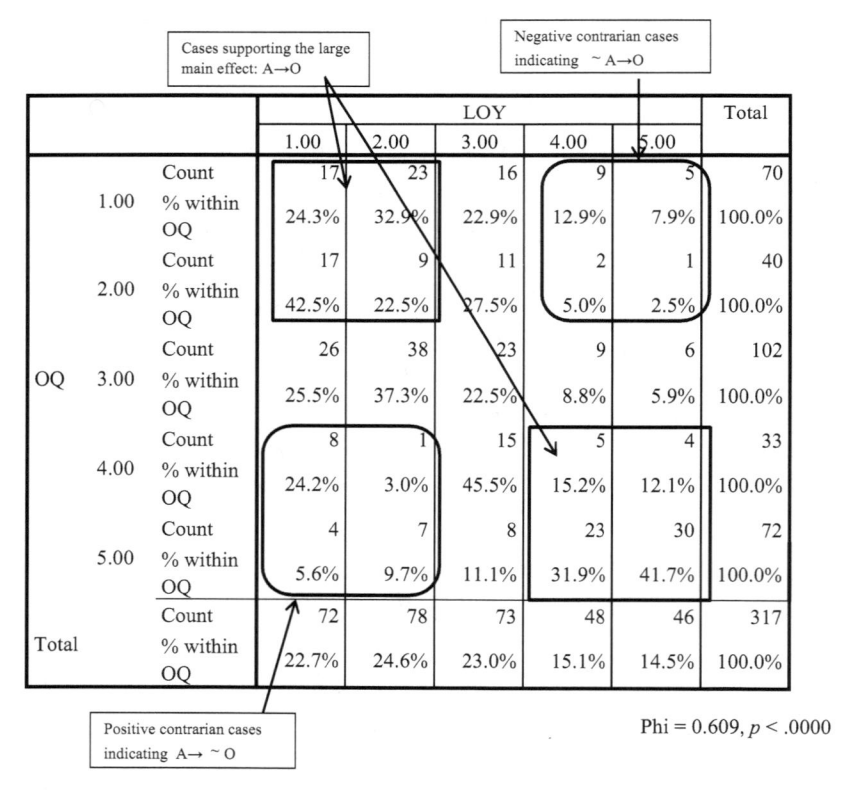

Figure 5.4 Two outcomes: offer quality (OQ) and customer loyalty (LOY)

Note: A = antecedent condition; O = outcome condition

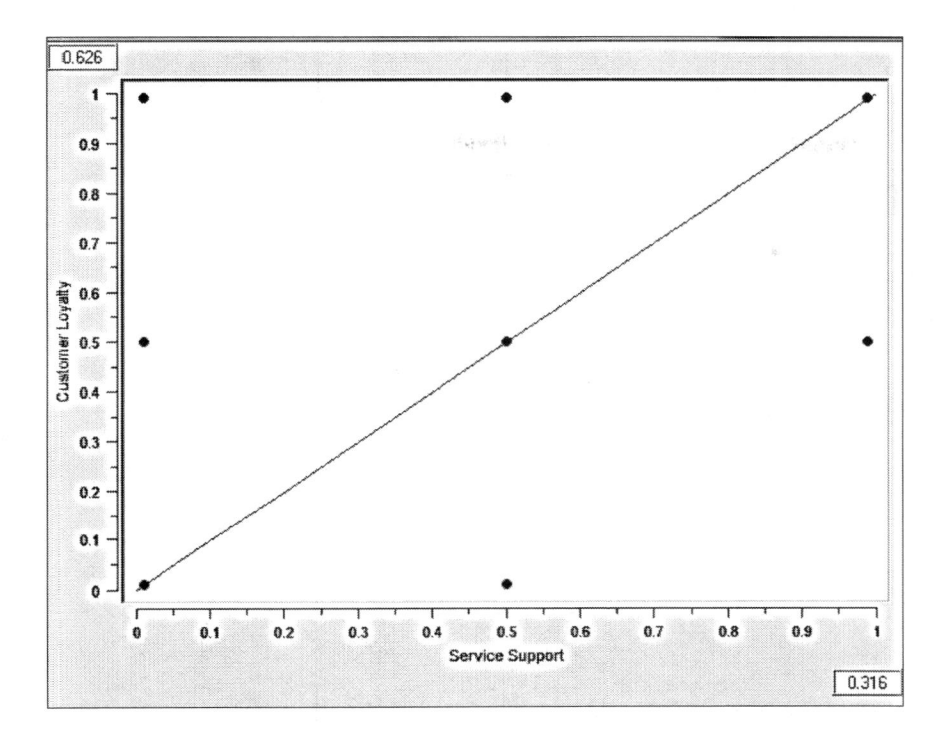

Figure 5.5 Asymmetric relationship between variables

to customer loyalty in Method 1 (MRA). Through the contingency table below (Figure 5.6) and the fuzzy XY plot (Figure 5.5), such results should be revised in light of the existence of several contrarian cases that demonstrated that such a relationship is 'asymmetric'.

In fact, such cases impact on the rest of the cases that constitute the large main effect (high values of X that lead to high values of Y and low values of X that lead to low values of Y). Consequently, when service support received a high evaluation by respondents, this attribute was not sufficient to create high loyalty (positive contrarian cases). Moreover, when respondents were not satisfied with the service support they received, this element did not necessarily affect and reduce their willingness to repurchase from the same company (negative contrarian cases).

This consideration can be applied to the other variables (antecedents) that were included in the regression models to understand whether their relationship with the outcome variables (in our case customer loyalty) is symmetric or not, and if there are contrarian cases. This analysis can be helpful for scholars to understand better the relationship among variables in their models.

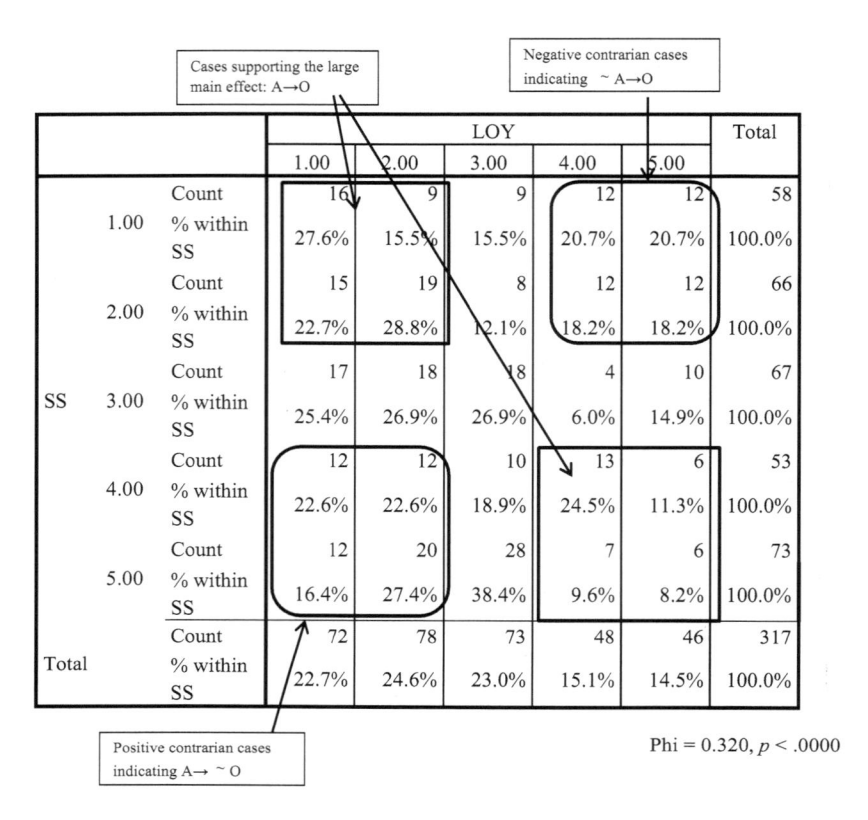

Figure 5.6 Two outcomes: service support (SS) and customer loyalty (LOY)

Note: A = antecedent condition; O = outcome condition

Procedure for qualitative comparative analysis

Following the results of the contrarian analysis, we can now apply complexity theory and configural analysis to our study to strive to enrich our understanding of the data. This is because we need not only to investigate the relationship between one single antecedent and the related outcome, but also to explore the existence of one or more combination/s of variables or dimensions that provide the same level of an outcome Y (in our study Y is customer loyalty). This is in line with configuration theory, which suggests that the same set of causal factors can lead to different outcomes, depending on how such factors are arranged (Ordanini et al., 2014).

This theory is based on three main principles that can be summarised as follows:

- an outcome of interest rarely results from a single causal variable
- causal variables rarely operate in isolation

- the same causal variable may have different effects (in same cases opposite) based on the context.

(Greckhamer et al., 2008)

Configural analysis helps in identifying and choosing only those configurations of variables that can effectively represent a phenomenon. These configurations can be more than one and this confirms the 'equifinality' tenent of complexity theory, which occurs when the same outcome can be achieved through different combinations of variables (Ragin, 2000). A tool that can helps scholars to screen and identify the right combinations of variables is fuzzy set QCA (fsQCA) software.[1] We adopted it for this study following the four-step procedure suggested by Fiss (2011), which we will explain in the following paragraph.

In contrast to statistical tools, QCA adopts a different terminology; for instance, it does not refer to an 'equation' but rather to a 'solution formula' or 'solution term' (Schneider and Wagemann, 2010). It is a set-theoretic method that empirically investigates the relationships between the outcome of interest (customer loyalty in our study) and all possible combinations of binary states (i.e., presence or absence) of its conditions (the independent variables; in our case we have, for instance, offer quality, personal interaction, service support, product specification) (Fiss, 2007; Ragin, 2000). QCA is based on the principles of set theory, formal logic, Boolean and fuzzy algebra, and it has gained more and more importance in management studies for its help in configurations analysis (Greckhamer, Misangyi, Elms and Lacey, 2007; Greckhamer et al., 2008; Chang, Tseng and Woodside, 2013; Leischnig and Kasper-Brauer, 2015; Ordanini et al., 2014; Russo et al., 2016; Ricciardi, Zardini and Rossignoli, 2016). Our aim is not to explain exhaustively the basis of such analysis from a theoretical and epistemological perspective, but rather to provide some examples of its usefulness and to suggest some guidelines to implement it from a management perspective. Initially, QCA was used for small samples (for instance between 15 and 40 cases), but recent studies have extended its application to larger samples, as suggested by previous research (e.g., Ragin and Fiss, 2008).

The steps that need to be followed to identify the 'recipe/s' of conditions (independent variables) that lead to a certain outcome (for us high levels of loyalty) are four (Figure 5.7):

In the first phase (*defining the property space*) QCA defines the property space, where all possible configurations of attributes of an outcome are identified. Decisions about the number of variables and their inclusion or exclusion are not random but should be employed with reference to the theoretical background of previous literature.

In our case, we identified our attributes from previous research as reported in the paragraph on 'measurement variables'. Defining the property space means to provide information about the combinations of attributes, consisting of all combinations of binary states (presense or absence) of the X attributes that could influence the outcome variables (ours is customer loyalty). These combinations are displayed in Figure 5.8, which is defined as a 'truth table'. The table

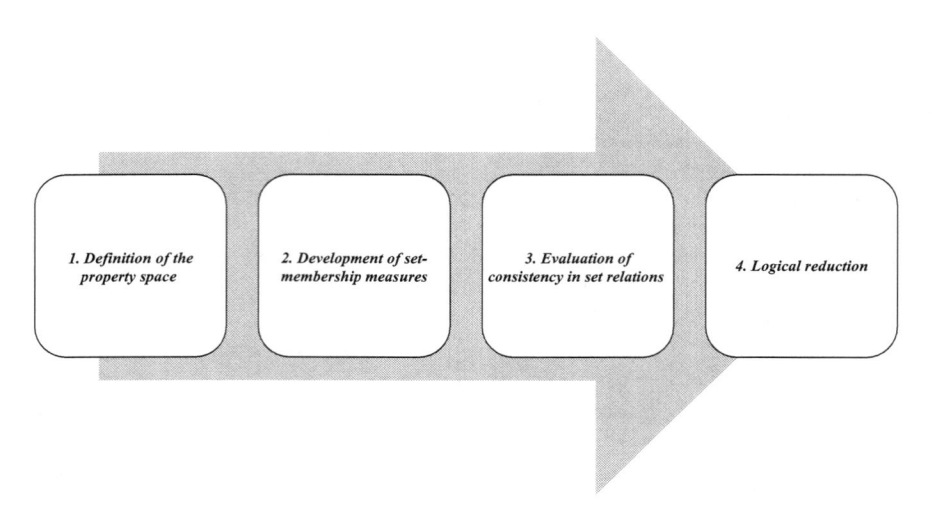

Figure 5.7 Steps for qualitative comparative analysis
Source: Our elaboration

shows the potential configuration of attributes in their combination of presence (high scores of X are assigned 1) or absence (low scores of X are assigned 0) in determining the outcome varible (high values of loyalty are assigned 1). The attributes we decided to adopt here for QCA analysis are offer quality (OQ), personal interaction (PI), service support (SS), product specification (product), percentage of expenditure with this supplier (expend) and length of partnership (partnership).

We exclude from the present analysis some attributes related to overall evaluation or perception, such as satisfaction and value perceived by customers, and perceived switching costs and product returns management, which we have already analysed in a previous manuscript (Russo et al., 2016). The aim here is to demonstrate how to use a method for data analysis and we do not strive at validating or testing specific theories or assumptions.

Following the first step, as suggested by Fiss (2007), we used these set measures to construct a data matrix (truth table) with 2^k rows, where k is the number of causal conditions (variables) used in the analysis. Each row of this table is associated with a specific combination of attributes, and the full table thus lists all possible combinations (for our study, we have $2^6 = 64$ combinations).

Some rows will contain more cases, some others very few and some rows could contain zero cases if there is no empirical evidence of such specific combinations of attributes.

Set-membership measures is the second phase of the analysis and consists of setting membership measures for the attributes. The conventional set (labelled the 'crisp' set) is dichotomous; that is, a case can be 'in' (present = 1) or 'out'

OQ	PI	SS	Product	Partnership	Expend	Number	Loy	Raw consist.	PRI consist.	SYM consist.
1	1	0	1	1	1	12		0.968620	0.928572	0.981132
0	1	1	0	1	0	8		0.888066	0.428575	1.000000
0	1	1	0	1	1	6		0.916049	0.700003	1.000000
1	0	0	1	0	1	2		1.000000	1.000000	1.000000
0	1	0	0	0	0	2		0.933851	0.333334	0.500000
1	1	1	1	0	0	1		1.000000	1.000000	1.000000
1	1	0	1	1	0	1		0.989525	0.960000	0.960000
1	1	0	0	1	1	1		0.968978	0.714286	0.833333
1	0	0	1	1	0	1		1.000000	1.000000	1.000000
1	0	0	1	0	0	1		0.984244	0.937500	0.937500
1	1	1	1	1	1	0				
1	1	1	1	1	0	0				
1	1	1	1	0	1	0				
1	1	1	0	1	1	0				
1	1	1	0	1	0	0				
1	1	1	0	0	1	0				
1	1	1	0	0	0	0				

Figure 5.8 Truth table of potential combinations

(absent = 0), while the fuzzy set membership scores can specify membership in the intervals between 0 and 1. For instance some are fully 'in' the set (fuzzy membership = 1.0), some are 'almost fully in' the set (membership = .90) and some are neither 'more in' nor 'more out' of the set (membership = .5, also known as the 'crossover point'). In our case we calibrated measures specifying three qualitative anchors: the threshold for full membership (1), the threshold for full non-membership (0) and a crossover point (0.5) (Ragin, 2008).

The endpoints and the midpoint of the seven-point Likert scales served as the three qualitative anchors for calibration of full membership (value 6), full non-membership (value 3) and the crossover point (value 4). Such calibration has been applied to the seven-point Likert scale constructs, which are: offer quality, personal interaction, product specification. Thus, for the variables related to the percentage of expenditure with the main supplier, the anchors were the following: the percentages of expenditure lower than 40% were transformed into 0 (non-membership), percentages between 40% and 60% were transformed into a crossover point (0.50) and percentages above were considered full membership (value 1). Meanwhile, for the length of partnership, relationships with the supplier that had lasted for less than one year were considered the threshold for full non-membership (0), the crossover point for half membership was at least one year until three years of partnership and the threshold for full membership (1) was considered above four years of partnership.

After generating fuzzy set measures for individual attributes by applying Boolean algebra rules, it is necessary to build membership scores for configurations. To allow replication, researchers should specify procedures for assigning fuzzy membership scores to cases, and these procedures must be both open and explicit so that they can be evaluated by other scholars. After showing all the numbers of rows and combinations, the table can be reduced, adopting two conditions: (1) the minimum number of cases required for a solution to be considered, and (2) the minimum consistency level of a solution (Ragin, 2008). 'Consistency' here refers to the degree to which cases correspond to the set-theoretic relationships expressed in a solution. This represents the third step: *consistency in set relations.*

Considering the minimum nuber of cases required to consider a solution, we considered the threshold of 1 (Ragin, 2008). The column 'number' of Table x shows the distribution of best-fit cases (customers) across the configurations in our sample.

We set the cases that led to high levels of loyalty; thus, we put loyalty as equal to 1, which represents when the outcome of high loyalty is present. For future research, scholars may also be interested in understanding those combinations that lead to low levels of an outcome, so the outcome variables should be fixed at 0, that is, an absence of the variable.

In both cases, this allows us to understand the number of potential combinations that lead to the same outcome. The next step is to consider only those combinations that satisfy the requirement of consistency. According to set theory, a consistent subset relation with fuzzy measures emerges when membership scores in a given causal set of attributes are consistently less than or equal to the membership scores in the outcome set. The consistency measure in this case is thus calculated as the sum of the consistent, or shared, membership scores in a causal set, divided by the sum of all the membership scores that pertain to that causal set. A configuration is accepted when its consistency measure exceeds a threshold, in line with QCA literature, of 0.80 (Ragin, 2008). From our elaboration, the most frequent and consistent combination seemed to be where all the conditions had high levels of satisfaction except for service support, which received low values (frequency = 12, raw consistency = 0.98). The second most consistent combination was the presence of high levels of personal interaction and a long partnership, which led to high levels of loyalty without having high levels of the other variables (frequency = 8, raw consistency = 0.91).

The last step is the *logical reduction and analysis of configuration*, which aims at identifying only those configurations that, beyond being consistent, also have an adequate level of coverage. Coverage explains the relevance of the combinations and it measures that share of consistent memberships as a proportion of the total membership in the outcome set. It can be interpreted as a sort of R-square value extracted from correlational methods (Woodside and Baxter, 2013). The accepted threshold for coverage is fixed at 0.10. Such an indicator provides researchers with support to assess the empirical relevance of configural statements. QCA calculates both raw and unique coverage scores, compared with raw, unique coverage controls for overlapping explanations by partitioning the raw coverage.

Findings from the qualitative comparative analysis

Table 5.5 shows the coverage and consistency of the six combinations that the software has selected to be 'sufficient' with the four steps following the above-described procedure. Ragin and Fiss (2008) have developed a useful way of presenting the results, in particular of fuzzy set analyses, according to which black circles ('●') indicate the presence of a condition and circles with a cross ('⊗') indicate its absence. Furthermore, a blank cell indicates the 'do not care' condition, which means a specific condition is not considered in a solution.

According to this approach, our study demonstrates the determination of high levels of customer loyalty through six solutions or 'recipes' (Table 5.5).

Solution 1 reflects a combination of the presence of offer quality, product specification and the absence of personal interaction, service support and length of partnership. This configuration represents the case where respondents are declared to be loyal when the core offering is satisfying, that is, the offering related to the product and core business of the company. Solution 2 combines the presence of personal interaction and service support and the length of partnership with the absence of offer quality and product specification, determining high levels of loyalty based on relationship and intangibles assets rather than on the core offering of products.

Table 5.5 Configurations for achieving high loyalty

Configurations	Solutions					
	1	2	3	4	5	6
Offer quality	●	⊗	●	●	⊗	●
Personal interaction	⊗	●		●	●	●
Product specification	●	⊗	●		⊗	●
Service support	⊗	●	⊗	⊗	⊗	●
Expenditure			⊗	●	⊗	⊗
Length of partnership	⊗	●	●	●	⊗	⊗
Consistency	0.99	0.85	0.98	0.96	0.93	1.00
Raw coverage	0.22	0.25	0.23	0.33	0.13	0.03
Unique coverage	0.03	0.22	0.07	0.17	0.03	0.01
Solution coverage	0.78					
Solution consistency	0.92					

Legend
● = Core causal condition present
⊗ = Core causal condition absent

Solution 3 includes the combination the previous two solutions, with the presence of offer quality, product specification and length of partnership but with the absence of service support and a high percentage of expenditure. Solution 4 adds to the third solution the presence of personal interaction and a great amount of expenditure with the main supplier. Such a solution is the most comprehensive of the key determinants of value and then loyalty. Solution 5 considers only the presence of personal interaction. Finally, solution 6 encompasses the presence of all the variables with the exception of expenditure and length of partnership. As can be noticed, the existence of multiple sufficient configurations for customer loyalty indicates equifinality (Fiss, 2011). Considering the coverage, the findings indicate an overall solution coverage of .78 and an overall consistency of .92, which indicate that a substantial proportion of the outcome is covered by the six configurations. Of the six configurations, solution 4 is the one with the highest raw coverage (value .33), highlighting that this combination of attributes provides the best representation of customer loyalty.

Study B. Measuring the impact of logistics service quality on customer loyalty

The second study that we present refers to the impact of LSQ perceptions on the intention to stay loyal to a firm. To assess and measure this phenomenon, we collected data from a global 3PL company that is a major player in the European 3PL food industry.[2] We adopted a quantitative methodology and data were collected via the survey method. The unit of analysis is represented by B2B companies that are customers of this 3PL company, and the sample company includes medium and large customers with different spending levels (see Table 5.7).

The food industry offers a high level of complexity because of the nature of the products, their conservation requirements (i.e., temperature, regulations) and the structure of the food market's logistics (frozen, fresh, fast food). The main services provided by the 3PL company included warehouse management, logistics and transportation of fresh and frozen products. Hence, this case is suitable for analysis through the lens of complexity theory in the following paragraphs. We will proceed as for the previous study (Study A), first describing the data collection and sample procedure steps and then analysing the data through two methods, first MRA and second QCA.

Data collection and survey development

Data collection relied on a Web-based survey on the Google Docs platform. After a pre-test refinement of the structure of the survey, the items were analysed and modified by a focus group comprising 10 logistics managers working for customer firms.

The link to the survey was mailed to 257 3PL customer firms and 150 completed surveys were returned. Respondents were asked to report their opinions about the services they received from their main 3PL provider and their intention to continue doing business with this provider. The survey was divided into three sections. The first section was constituted by questions related to the *demographic characteristics* of the customer firms (e.g., size, typology of logistics and transportation services they received from the 3PL company, the length of the partnership with this service provider, the role of the respondents in their company).

The second section aimed at evaluating seven multi-item constructs constituting the LSQ scale (e.g., personnel contact quality, information quality, order procedure, order accuracy, order condition, order discrepancy, timeliness). All the scales were taken and adapted from previous research (see Table 5.6). All

Table 5.6 Measurement of variables

	Items	References
LSQ Scale		Rafiq and Jaafar (2007)
Personnel contact quality	3	Mentzer, Flint and Hult (2001)
Information quality	5	Rafiq and Jaafar (2007)
Ordering procedures	6	Rafiq and Jaafar (2007)
Order accuracy	3	Mentzer et al. (2001)
Order condition	3	Mentzer et al. (2001)
Order discrepancy handling	4	Extended from Mentzer et al. (2001)
Timeliness	3	Mentzer et al. (2001)

items were evaluated on a seven-point Likert scale following Rafiq and Jaafar (2007) (1 = highly dissatisfied, 7 = highly satisfied).

The third section, covering intention to continue doing business with the company, was measured using a three-item construct (Molinari, Abratt and Dion, 2008).

Sample characteristics

One hundred and fifty completed surveys were collected and encompassed a wide range of companies that are customers of the 3PL company. Such companies have been classified into three clusters (Table 5.7): (1) large customers, which are large in terms of their volume and revenue (36% of the sample); (2) retailers (3%); and (3) medium customers, in terms of their volume and revenue (61%).

Most respondents were logistics-related managers (49%; see Table 5.8), which implies the likely reliability of the information obtained, because these respondents should have a high level of familiarity with the subject matter and can appropriately assess the logistics services provided by their 3PL providers.

Method 1. Multiple regression analysis

To analyse the data, first we provide some descriptive statistics and correlation analysis of LSQ drivers. Then, we run a linear regression model to explore the

Table 5.7 Sample companies

Clusters	n.	Percentage
Large	54	36%
Retailers	5	3%
Medium	91	61%
Total	150	100%

Table 5.8 Respondents

Respondents	n.	Percentage
Owner/CEO	12	8%
Supply chain manager	11	7%
Logistics manager	73	49%
Procurement manager	5	3%
Sales manager	11	7%
Accounting manager	4	3%
Other	34	23%
Total	150	100%

impact of the LSQ drivers on customer loyalty. Table 5.9 presents the minimum, maximum, means and standard deviation of the selected variables. On average, personal contact quality represents the dimension with which respondents were most satisfied (mean = 5.33), followed by order procedures (mean = 5.00). Regarding the dependent variables, the average mean is 4.531. Overall, all the dimensions have an average score that is beyond 4.

Considering the correlation analysis among the variables, we found that all the variables are correlated (Table 5.10). However, only a few relationships have a coefficient that exceeds $r > 0.6$ (information quality with ordering procedures, information quality with order discrepancy, order accuracy with order condition, order condition with timeliness).

To assess reliability, we first tested for internal consistency. The normalised Cronbach's alpha took a value of 0.75, exceeding the minimum value of 0.7. We also determined the Cronbach's alpha values for each item, to confirm whether excluding any items might improve the overall alpha. After descriptive statistics

Table 5.9 Descriptive statistics

	Min	Max	Median	Mean	St. Dev.
Personnel contact quality	1	7	5.330	5.191	1.248
Information quality	1	7	4.600	4.587	1.227
Ordering procedures	1	7	5.000	4.797	1.039
Order accuracy	1	7	4.667	4.422	1.532
Order condition	1	7	4.667	4.602	1.252
Order discrepancy handling	1	7	4.250	4.152	1.180
Timeliness	1	7	4.333	4.276	1.248
Customer loyalty	1	7	4.625	4.531	1.186

Table 5.10 Correlation analysis

	1	2	3	4	5	6	7	8
1. Personnel contact quality	1							
2. Information quality	0.576**	1						
3. Ordering procedures	0.653**	0.551**	1					
4. Order accuracy	0.479**	0.474**	0.531**	1				
5. Order condition	0.570**	0.498**	0.556**	0.690**	1			
6. Order discrepancy handling	0.510**	0.638**	0.524**	0.391**	0.511**	1		
7. Timelines	0.531**	0.442**	0.511**	0.597**	0.637**	0.504**	1	
8. Customer loyalty	0.598**	0.526**	0.619**	0.446**	0.577**	0.518**	0.610**	1

** Correlation is significant at the 0.01 level

Table 5.11 Regression analysis for customer loyalty

	Estimate	Std. Error	t value	Pr(> |t|)
(Constant)	.290	.342	.848	.398
Personnel contact quality	.147	.079	1.776	.078
Information quality	.113	.079	1.386	.168
Ordering procedure	.258	.093	3.155	.002
Order accuracy	−.124	.065	−1.486	.139
Order condition	.167	.085	1.870	.064
Order discrepancy handling	.052	.080	.658	.512
Timeliness	.291	.070	3.639	.000

Signif. codes: 0 '***' 0.001 '**' 0.01 '*' 0.05 '.' 0.1 ' ' 1
Multiple R-squared: .553, Adjusted R-squared: .531

and reliability tests, we analysed data through the following regression model. Data were elaborated using *R* software.

$$\begin{aligned}
Customer\,loyalty = {}& \beta_0 + \beta_1\,Personnel\,Contact\,Quality \\
& + \beta_2\,Information\,Quality + \beta_3\,Ordering\,Procedures \\
& + \beta_4\,Order\,Accuracy + \beta_5\,Order\,Condition \\
& + \beta_6\,Order\,Discrepancy\,Handling + \beta_7\,Timeliness + \varepsilon.
\end{aligned} \tag{2}$$

Considering the relationship among the independent variables and customer loyalty, we found that very few variables have a positive and significant relationship (Table 5.11). These are ordering procedures ($\beta = .2$, p value $< .01$) and timeliness ($\beta = .291$, p value $< .001$). Thus, high values of these variables will lead to high levels of customer loyalty, while low values of ordering procedures or timeliness will lead to low values of customer loyalty. It is not surprising that time represents a key element when considering a logistics-specific scenario. This study leads to evaluate logistics service and what emerges is that, despite all the elements that can enhance customer loyalty, time is the main determinant along with the satisfaction with the procedures related to the order.

It appears that very few variables have a single, direct and significant effect on loyalty. Maybe through Method 2, a better understanding of this lack of significance can be provided. Overall, the model has an R^2 of .553 and adjusted R^2 of .531. The main results are reported in Table 5.11.

Method 2. Qualitative comparative analysis using fuzzy set qualitative comparative analysis software

Adopting the same approach as study A, the first step to conduct is to consider whether there is the presence of asymmetric relationships among some antecedents and the outcome variables, with the existence of contrarian cases. Following the same procedure through SPSS cross-tabulation, we related each of the independent variables to our dependent variable, the customer loyalty. We did not found any relevant cases of contrarian cases, while most of the large main effects

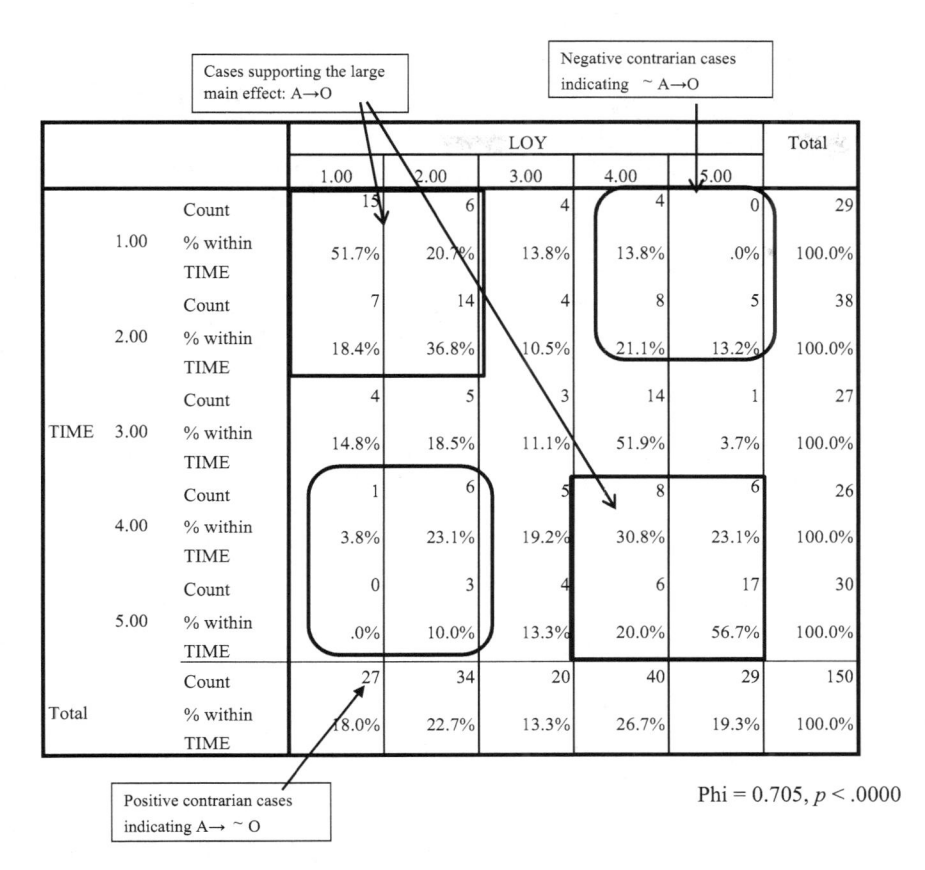

Figure 5.9 Two outcomes: timeliness (TIME) and customer loyalty (LOY)

Note: A = antecedent condition; O = outcome condition

were confirmed. Here, Figure 5.9 reports the example of timeliness constructs related to customer loyalty. What emerges is that cases supporting the large main effects are more frequent than negative or positive contrarian cases. This confirms the significant and positive effect of timeliness on loyalty in Method 1 (MRA).

Procedure for qualitative comparative analysis

Applying QCA, we present here some findings to probe the existence of causal recipe antecedents associations with the outcome condition and to present an examination of the influence of LSQ on customer loyalty. In the first phase (*defining the property space*), QCA defines the property space, where all possible configurations of attributes (present or absent) of an outcome are identified.

These combinations are displayed in Figure 5.10, which is defined as the truth table. The attributes we decided to adopt for QCA analysis are personnel

Personnel	Info	Procedures	Accuracy	Condition	Discrepancy	Timeliness	Number	Loyalty	Raw consist.	PRI consist.	SYM consist.
0	0	0	0	0	0	0	8		0.618241	0.055556	0.057143
1	1	1	1	1	1	1	2		0.887208	0.720000	0.720000
1	1	1	1	1	0	0	1		0.903321	0.571428	0.571429
1	1	1	1	1	1	0	0				
1	1	1	1	1	0	1	0				
1	1	1	1	0	1	1	0				
1	1	1	1	0	1	0	0				
1	1	1	1	0	0	1	0				
1	1	1	1	0	0	0	0				

Figure 5.10 Truth table

contact quality, information quality, ordering procedure, order accuracy, order condition, order discrepancy handling, timeliness. The truth table shows all the combination of attributes; in this case we obtained $2^7 = 128$ combinations. However, only three rows contain valid cases, highlighting the existence of three possible combinations.

The second phase of the analysis (*set-membership measures*) calibrated the measures based on their membership or non-membership. We adopted the same thresholds of the previous case study: the threshold for full membership (1), the threshold for full non-membership (0) and a crossover point (0.5) (Ragin, 2008). The three qualitative anchors for calibration of full membership were also fixed here within the seven-point Likert scale: full membership (value 6), full non-membership (value 3) and the crossover point (value 4).

We then assessed our configurations in terms of *consistency in set relations* (third phase). The column 'number' in Figure 5.10 shows the distribution of best-fit cases (customers) across the configurations in our sample. We selected the cases that lead to high levels of loyalty, so we put loyalty as equal to 1, that is, when the outcome of high loyalty is present.

Because a configuration is accepted when its consistency measure exceeds a threshold of 0.80 (Ragin, 2008), we had to accept only two configurations out of three. The last step is *logical reduction and analysis of configuration*, which aims at identifying only those configurations that are beyond being consistent and that also have an adequate level of coverage.

Findings from the qualitative comparative analysis

Table 5.12 shows the coverage and consistency of the two combinations that the software selected to be 'sufficient' with the four steps following the above-described procedure. In this case, we have only two 'recipes' that create high levels of loyalty. In line with the layout suggested by Ragin and Fiss (2008), black circles represent the present of the involved condition while circles with the cross out represent those condition which are absent in the specific recipe. In addition to this, as it can be noticed from the table, some circles are bigger than others. These latter ones represent the "core conditions" that are included in the parsimonious solutions that must be included in any representation of the results, as they are the decisive causal ingredients. Conversely, smaller circles represent peripheral conditions within a recipe.

Solution 1 reflects a combination where respondents declared their loyalty when personnel contact quality, information quality, ordering procedure, order accuracy and order condition were satisfying, while order discrepancy handling and timeliness were not. Solution 2 sees the presence of all the configurations, showing the importance of a full combination of ingredients to achieve loyalty.

Here, QCA is useful as it confirms a tenet of complexity theory, specifically tenet 1: 'A simple antecedent condition may be necessary but a simple antecedent condition is rarely sufficient for predicting a high or low score in an outcome condition'. This determines that a single variable rarely leads to high levels

Table 5.12 Configurations for achieving high loyalty

Configurations Solutions		
	1	2
Personal contact quality	●	●
Information quality	●	●
Ordering procedure	●	●
Order accuracy	●	●
Order condition	●	●
Order discrepancy handling	⊗	•
Timeliness	⊗	•
Consistency	0.903	0.376
Raw coverage	0.383	0.143
Unique coverage	0.150	0.887
Solution coverage	0.53	
Solution consistency	0.90	

Legend
● = Core causal condition present
⊗ = Core causal condition absent

of loyalty (as Method 1 confirmed through regression analysis). In contrast, a full recipe of predictors is necessary, or of most of them, supporting tenet 2.

Final comment

To summarise, QCA is particularly useful for several objectives. It can been adopted alone or, even better, in combination with more conventional methods. It can help to summarise data and to text hypotheses and theories. Moreover, it can provide a better overview about data and relationships among variables. In addition, based on results derived from such analyses, QCA is helpful in delivering inputs for the development of new theoretical arguments.

From our experience, QCA should be applied together with other data analysis techniques in a complementary way, especially if the aim is to draw causal inferences. In fact, it offers scholars a meaningful interpretation of results, being more precise compared with statistical methods in highlighting the existence of differences between cases and in clustering different paths towards an outcome. Such methodologies (mixed methods) can deliver added value and they can include multiple methods in a step-wise progression (for instance choosing a qualitative method first, followed by a quantitative method, or selecting the same method adopted in different steps). Nevertheless, a disadvantage of such an approach is that, generally, multi-method studies must deal with very restrictive space limitations required by journal articles. However, in the case that QCA is the only method used, it is important to report step by step the research process that generated the data and to remind the reader which other methods (both qualitative as case studies, or quantitative as statistical analyses) should be applied in subsequent analyses, and why.

Notes

1 For further information about the usage and guidelines of fsQCA, please visit the website: www.u.arizona.edu/~cragin/fsQCA/.
2 We deeply thank our colleague Barbara Gaudenzi for allowing us to share these data we collected during a project of which she was the leader (Russo, Gaudenzi, Confente and Borghesi, 2015).

References

Anderson, P. (1999) 'Perspective: complexity theory and organization science', *Organization Science*, 10(3), 216–232.

Armstrong, J. S. (2011) *Illusions in regression analysis*. Available at SSRN 1969740.

Barile, S. and Polese, F. (2010) 'Smart service systems and viable service systems: applying systems theory to service science', *Service Science*, 2(1–2), 21–40.

Berry, L. L. and Bendapudi, N. (2007) 'Health care a fertile field for service research', *Journal of Service Research*, 10(2), 111–122.

Blocker, C. P. (2011) 'Modeling customer value perceptions in cross-cultural business markets', *Journal of Business Research*, 64(5), 533–540.

Blocker, C. P., Flint, D. J., Myers, M. B. and Slater, S. F. (2011) 'Proactive customer orientation and its role for creating customer value in global markets', *Journal of the Academy of Marketing Science*, 39(2), 216–233.

Byrne, D. and Callaghan, G. (2013) Complexity theory and the social sciences: the state of the art, New York: Routledge.

Chang, C. W., Tseng, T. H. and Woodside, A. G. (2013) 'Configural algorithms of patient satisfaction, participation in diagnostics, and treatment decisions' influences on hospital loyalty', *Journal of Services Marketing*, 27(2), 91–103.

Choi, T. Y. and Krause, D. R. (2006) 'The supply base and its complexity: implications for transaction costs, risks, responsiveness, and innovation', *Journal of Operations Management*, 24(5), 637–652.

Crié, D. and Chebat, J. C. (2013) 'Health marketing: toward an integrative perspective', *Journal of Business Research*, 66(1), 123–126.

Fiss, P. C. (2007) 'A set-theoretic approach to organizational configurations', *Academy of Management Review*, 32(4), 1180–1198.

Fiss, P. C. (2011) 'Building better causal theories: a fuzzy set approach to typologies in organization research', *Academy of Management Journal*, 54(2), 393–420.

Flint, D. J., Blocker, C. P. and Boutin Jr., P. J. (2011) 'Customer value anticipation, customer satisfaction and loyalty: an empirical examination', *Industrial Marketing Management*, 40(2), 219–230.

Gigerenzer, G. (1991) 'How to make cognitive illusions disappear: beyond "heuristics and biases"', *European Review of Social Psychology*, 2(1), 83–115.

Gigerenzer, G. and Brighton, H. (2009) 'Homo heuristicus: why biased minds make better inferences', *Topics in Cognitive Science*, 1(1), 107–143.

Gladwell, M. (2006) The tipping point: how little things can make a big difference, New York: Little, Brown.

Greckhamer, T., Misangyi, V. F., Elms, H. and Lacey, R. (2007) 'Using qualitative comparative analysis in strategic management research: An examination of combinations of industry, corporate, and business-unit effects', *Organizational Research Methods*, 11(4), 1–32.

Greckhamer, T., Misangyi, V. F., Elms, H. and Lacey, R. (2008) 'Using qualitative comparative analysis in strategic management research: An examination of combinations of industry, corporate, and business-unit effects', *Organizational Research Methods*, 11(4), 695–726.

Gummesson, E. (2008) 'Extending the service-dominant logic: from customer centricity to balanced centricity', *Journal of the Academy of Marketing Science*, 36(1), 15–17.

Hsiao, J. P. H., Jaw, C., Huan, T. C. and Woodside, A. G. (2015) 'Applying complexity theory to solve hospitality contrarian case conundrums: illuminating happy-low and unhappy-high performing frontline service employees', *International Journal of Contemporary Hospitality Management*, 27(4), 608–647.

Lam, S. Y., Shankar, V., Erramilli, M. K. and Murthy, B. (2004) 'Customer value, satisfaction, loyalty, and switching costs: an illustration from a business-to-business service context', *Journal of the Academy of Marketing Science*, 32(3), 293–311.

Leischnig, A. and Kasper-Brauer, K. (2015) 'Employee adaptive behavior in service enactments', *Journal of Business Research*, 68(2), 273–280.

Levy, D. (1994) 'Chaos theory and strategy: theory, application and managerial implications', *Strategic Management Journal*, 15, 167–178.

Manuj, I. and Sahin, F. (2011) 'A model of supply chain and supply chain decision-making complexity', *International Journal of Physical Distribution & Logistics Management*, 41(5), 511–549.

McClelland, D. C. (1998) 'Identifying competencies with behavioral-event interviews', *Psychological Science*, 9, 331–339.

Mele, C. and Polese, F. (2011) 'Key dimensions of service systems in value-creating networks', in H. Demirkan, J. Spohrer and V. Krishna (eds), *The science of service systems*, New York: Springer, 37–59.

Mentzer, J. T., Flint, D. J. and Hult, G. T. M. (2001) 'Logistics service quality as a segment-customized process', *Journal of Marketing*, 65(4), 82–104.

Molinari, L. K., Abratt, R. and Dion, P. (2008) 'Satisfaction, quality and value and effects on repurchase and positive word-of-mouth behavioral intentions in a B2B services context', *Journal of Services Marketing*, 22(5), 363–373.

Mollenkopf, D. A., Rabinovich, E., Laseter, T. M. and Boyer, K. K. (2007) 'Managing internet product returns: a focus on effective service operations', *Decision Sciences*, 38(2), 215–250.

Ordanini, A., Parasuraman, A. and Rubera, G. (2014) 'When the recipe is more important than the ingredients: a qualitative comparative analysis (QCA) of service innovation configurations', *Journal of Service Research*, 17, 134–149.

Rafiq, M. and Jaafar, H. S. (2007) 'Measuring customers' perceptions of logistics service quality of 3pl service providers', *Journal of Business Logistics*, 28(2), 159–175.

Ragin, C. C. (2000) *Fuzzy set social science*, Chicago, IL: University of Chicago Press.

Ragin, C. C. (2008) *Redesigning social inquiry: fuzzy sets and beyond* (Vol. 240), Chicago, IL: University of Chicago Press.

Ragin, C. C. and Fiss, P. C. (2008) 'Net effects analysis versus configurational analysis: an empirical demonstration', in C. C. Ragin (ed), *Redesigning social inquiry: fuzzy sets and beyond*, 190–212. Thousand Oaks, CA: Sage.

Ricciardi, F., Zardini, A. and Rossignoli, C. (2016) 'Organizational dynamism and adaptive business model innovation: the triple paradox configuration', *Journal of Business Research*, 69(11), 5487–5493.

Russo, I., Confente, I., Gligor, D. M. and Autry, C. W. (2016) 'To be or not to be (loyal): is there a recipe for customer loyalty in the B2B context?', *Journal of Business Research*, 69(2), 888–896.

Russo, I., Gaudenzi, B., Confente, I. and Borghesi, A. (2015) 'Logistics service quality: searching for new drivers of 3PL customers' satisfaction', in Zhang, Z., Shen, Z., Zhang, J., and Zhang R. (eds), *LISS 2014*, 383–387. Springer, Berlin: Heidelberg.

Schneider, C. Q. and Wagemann, C. (2010) 'Standards of good practice in qualitative comparative analysis (QCA) and fuzzy-sets', *Comparative Sociology*, 9(3), 397–418.

Simon, H. A. (1962) 'The architecture of complexity', *Proceedings of the American Philosophical Society*, 106(6), 467–482.

Simon, H. A. (1996) *The sciences of the artificial*, Cambridge, MA: MIT press.

Sterman, J. D. and Wittenberg, J. (1999) 'Path dependence, competition, and succession in the dynamics of scientific revolution', *Organization Science*, 10(3), 322–341.

Ulaga, W. and Eggert, A. (2006) 'Value-based differentiation in business relationships: gaining and sustaining key supplier status', *Journal of Marketing*, 70(1), 119–136.

Urry, J. (2005). 'The complexity turn', *Theory, Culture & Society*, 22(5), 1–14. London, Thousand Oaks and New Delhi: SAGE.

Woodside, A. G. (2014) 'Embrace•perform•model: complexity theory, contrarian case analysis, and multiple realities', *Journal of Business Research*, 67(12), 2495–2503.

Woodside, A. G. (2015) 'Constructing business-to-business marketing models that overcome the limitations in variable-based and case-based research paradigms', *Journal of Business-to-Business Marketing*, 22(1–2), 95–110.

Woodside, A. G. and Baxter, R. (2013) 'Achieving accuracy, generalization-to-contexts, and complexity in theories of business-to-business decision processes', *Industrial Marketing Management*, 42(3), 382–393.

Wu, P.-L., Yeh, S.-S., Huan, T. C. and Woodside, A. G. (2014) 'Applying complexity theory to deepen service dominant logic: configural analysis of customer experience-and-outcome assessments of professional services for personal transformations', *Journal of Business Research*, 67(8), 1647–1670.

6 Concluding thoughts and future research

The starting perspective of our book was from under a B2B marketing umbrella; however, in the context of B2B, because firms enter into relationships with suppliers, wholesalers, retailers, service providers and customers, we decided to integrate this perspective with the domain of supply chain management. In fact, one of marketing's main concerns is delivering value to the final customer, but an inefficiency or mistake anywhere within the supply chain (i.e., products out of stock, poor performance by a 3PL, damaged goods, longer lead time, returns products) can have a significantly negative effect on the final result. Therefore, this might reduce customer satisfaction and loyalty. Thus, we proposed to analyse the dimension of customer loyalty adopting a strong integration between supply chain performances and marketing results in enhancing this dimension.

In essence, our book provides evidence that customer loyalty cannot be accurately explained without acknowledging the complex reality in which this variable manifests itself, particularly in a supply chain context. Business scholars have long proposed that firms with a good understanding of the sources of customer loyalty can gain market advantages such as increased revenues, lower costs and increased profitability, to name a few. Successful firms have realised the importance of customer loyalty, and are investing significant resources in customer retention, investigating both customer attitude and customer behaviour. In parallel, competition among enterprises has evolved with the result that supply chains compete against each other because the challenge is not only to serve the global customer in the best way possible but also to select the best suppliers. Globalisation has set up large systems of trading partners that span vast distances, different cultures, several operational risks and increased complexity. Those dynamics affect the efficiency (i.e., cost reduction, quality) and effectiveness (i.e., customer service, delivery time) of supply chains designed to create time, place and form utility to improve the customers' commitment. In considering the challenges the firm faces with respect to global supply chains, demand and supply integration (DSI) provides a basis for understanding the problems the firm faces, as well as a means for guiding future research with respect to customer loyalty within the global context. The complexity also requires inter-functional integration between marketing, sales, logistics, operations, accounting, finance and legal within a firm, and inter-firm coordination across the supply chain.

This is helpful to balance demand and supply constraints, capabilities and opportunities. The ability to create value often rests on the necessity of cross-functional integration and collaboration across the supply chain to improve the level of trust, commitment, LSQ and satisfaction. This requires firms to transcend the functional silos, shifting towards a cross-functional approach to value creation. These are relevant issues when looking for the most appropriate recipe to keep customers loyal. Future research needs to be especially focused on aspects of functional integration and DSI with respect to customer loyalty. Moreover, we invite scholars to explore more broadly the role of individuals across multiple functions in supplier and customer organisations who engage in creating a higher commitment.

In the real world, relationships between variables can be non-linear, so it was important to show how firms participating in B2B markets can achieve high levels of customer loyalty under different configurations of several variables. We have provided the reader with several examples in the previous chapters. Starting with more 'standard approaches', using MRA we gave some empirical examples of how loyalty has been affected by multiple drivers. Our aim was not to include all the possible statistical methods that the literature usually adopts to investigate such relationships, so we are aware that other ones could be used to provide a richer examination of linear relationships. SEM is one such method, and one of the most used in the literature, so scholars could also consider this approach when making a comparison between symmetric and asymmetric relationships.

After this, we contextualised the most recent methodological techniques to capture better the complexity under which firms must operate, giving some examples of data analysis that provide combinations of antecedents that lead to loyalty. In brief, the relationships between customer loyalty antecedents and loyalty can be non-linear with abrupt switches, and the same antecedent can, in certain circumstances, have a different impact on a specific outcome. To demonstrate this, we adopted contrarian analysis, which highlights the existence of contrarian cases that have opposite results on the same outcome. As such, our results indicate that despite the long tradition of customer loyalty research, because of the past methodologies employed and the complexity of the phenomenon, significant work remains to be done to develop a better understanding of how firms can achieve customer loyalty across the supply chain.

This book also shows how firms can achieve high levels of customer loyalty under different configurations of loyalty constructs in a supply chain context. In doing so, we selected some antecedents and we analysed through the QCA approach the existence of several solutions that lead to high levels of customer loyalty. Then, we are aware that our intent was to demonstrate only how to adopt and use this method and not to be exhaustive in including all the possible antecedents of customer loyalty. As such, one limitation of our study is that we considered a limited number of factors linking with the products flow that can affect customer loyalty. Future research could consider other possible combinations and explore how the impact of these antecedents on customer loyalty changes when other variables are considered.

Complexities can arise when the customer-supplier relationship involves an overabundance of exchanged goods and services with varying levels of switching costs and service. We avoided discussing the role of incentive programmes in building loyalty because relational strategies such as LSQ or value creation have better results, as we have demonstrated in our book. Future research should attempt to develop a better understanding of how inter-product and inter-service dependencies would impact the relationships examined in the current study.

Qualitative research could help reveal a more in-depth perspective regarding the relationships of interest, exploring mechanisms and contexts related to why, how and when customer satisfaction leads to customer loyalty, and then related to firms' financial performance. This confirms another limitation of this book, as we did not include a demonstration of 'standard' qualitative methods (i.e., case study or grounded theory) that are useful to analyse a deep and complex phenomenon of customer loyalty. If future scholars were to do so, they could show how results from interviews can also be elaborated and analysed through QCA. Few studies have already done such analysis and a very recent research provided a major contribution on how conducting qualitative comparative analysis starting from interviews' results (Forkmann et al., 2017). Consistent with complexity theory, future research employing a qualitative approach could better understand the complexity within which the phenomenon of customer loyalty manifests itself and how to anticipate the first silent disloyal signals. Such an approach could further aid future research because it could help identify additional potential antecedents or factors that impact customer loyalty and disloyalty.

We also encourage future research that would unpack the complex interactions between value, satisfaction and attitudinal or behavioural loyalty to understand better the different recipes for different segments of customers. The value of loyalty to a supplier depends on the composition of the customers and their relative level of loyalty. Therefore, it could be helpful for managers to understand different customer types and to develop specific strategies for managing customers. Longitudinal research could help reveal a more in-depth perspective regarding the relationships of interest and how loyal customers change over the time.

Future research ought to replicate this study's findings and method across emerging markets to establish further the validity of the method. In connection with this, research stream results may be different in countries with unique cultures, habits and business practices. Accordingly, research should be undertaken to gain more understanding of B2B loyalty effects associated with switching cost perceptions and suppliers' capabilities with respect to national characteristics and cultural distance in the context of the global market.

With the particular attention it pays to the rapid emergence of omnichannel retailing, we hope this book can contribute to the existing literature on customer loyalty. The presence of online versus offline marketing channels has increased the importance of discovering how to manage supply chains effectively across different retail channels and of addressing consumers' emerging needs.

It would be interesting to consider the dynamic environments in which most firms operate. Moreover, it would be interesting to examine the role of the new technologies in the era of Industry 4.0 to build smart supply chain networks. Therefore, scholars interested in collaborative supply chain technologies should explore the potential benefits of increasing the variety of technology collaborations using business analytic tools.

In addition, from a customer perspective, the growing complexity across the supply chain is particularly salient as omnichannel retailing evolves to include more consumer touchpoints that demand building smart and fit strategies into the supply chain. This includes building relationships between suppliers and customers in the B2B context, with a major focus on end-to-end integration, from the supplier's supplier to the customers' customer. The consumer, who will buy, use and wear the product, is the last aspect of supply chain integration. Thus, supplier-manufacturer-customer relationships are crucial to the success of shopper marketing execution, requiring a rethink of supply chain design, logistics network distribution and inventory management, from both consumer and supply chain perspectives. Future research needs to investigate how to integrate research on loyalty in the B2B context with consumer loyalty; one of the most intriguing aspects of future research will be a comparative approach to customer loyalty in B2B and B2C contexts, which could lead to cross-fertilisation between the two areas, with each retaining its own features.

Reference

Forkmann, S., Henneberg, S. C., Witell, L., & Kindström, D. (2017). Driver Configurations for Successful Service Infusion. *Journal of Service Research*, in press, doi: 10.1177/1094670517706160 .

Index